A NATURAL HISTORY OF THE CORAL REEF

Lagoon of a small coral atoll

CHARLES R.C. SHEPPARD

A
NATURAL HISTORY
OF THE
CORAL REEF

BLANDFORD PRESS

POOLE DORSET

First published in the U.K. 1983 by Blandford Press
Link House, West Street, Poole, Dorset, BH15 1LL

Copyright © 1983 Blandford Books Ltd

ISBN 0 7137 1268 6

14905 Blandford Press

British Library Cataloguing in Publication Data

Sheppard, Charles R.C.
  A natural history of the Coral reef.
  1. Coral reef biology
  I. Title
  574.909′42   QH95.8

Typeset in 10/12 pt Monophoto Baskerville
by Asco Trade Typesetting Ltd., Hong Kong
Printed by South China Printing Co., Hong Kong

CONTENTS

ACKNOWLEDGEMENTS

Grateful acknowledgement is made to the following for permission to reproduce photographic material:
Aquavisuals Ltd: pp. 10*b*, 49*t*, 49*b*, 67*tl*, 74*t*, 80*l*, 83*t*, 83*b*, 89*b*, 98*b*, 101, 102*t*, 102*b*, 103*b*; Mike Ballantyne: pp. 23*t*, 67*b*; Bruce Chalker: pp. 9*b*, 37*b*, 39*r*, 55*t*, 59*t*, 62*t*, 66, 78*t*, 90*t*, 121, 124; Brian Dawkins: p. 70*t*; Ed Drew: p. 41*b*; David George: p. 19*m*; Mont Hirons: p. 138*b*; David Hopley: p. 17; Ed Lovell: pp. 4, 18, 35*t*, 46*t*, 47, 48*t*, 57*t*, 61*b*, 63*b*, 64*b*, 70*m*, 70*b*, 74*b*, 79*t*, 79*b*, 90*b*, 93*b*, 142, 144; Peter Ormerod: pp. 97, 120*l*, 128*b*, 131; D.R. Robertson: p. 86*t*; Gary Russ: p. 55*bl*; Anne Sheppard: pp. 3*b*, 8*t*, 8*b*, 9*t*, 14, 19*t*, 19*b*, 22*t*, 23*bl*, 23*br*, 24*t*, 24*m*, 24*b*, 29*t*, 29*b*, 30, 34, 35*b*, 37*t*, 38*l*, 39*tl*, 46*b*, 48*b*, 58*t*, 58*b*, 60, 63*b*, 63*tr*, 64*t*, 71*t*, 75*t*, 75*b*, 78*b*, 80*r*, 89*t*, 91*t*, 91*b*, 94*t*, 94*b*, 95, 96*t*, 96*b*, 100*t*, 106*t*, 109, 111*r*, 114*t*, 115*t*, 118*t*, 119*t*, 119*bl*, 120*rt*, 120*rb*, 122*t*, 122*b*, 130*b*, 143*l*; Charles Sheppard: pp. ii, 3*t*, 11*t*, 11*b*, 22*m*, 22*b*, 25, 26*l*, 26*r*, 27*l*, 27*r*, 27*b*, 28*t*, 28*b*, 38*r*, 39*b*, 41*t*, 43, 44, 45, 57*b*, 71*b*, 77*t*, 77*b*, 82*t*, 86*bl*, 86*br*, 87, 93*t*, 98*t*, 100*b*, 104, 111*l*, 115*b*, 119*br*, 126*t*, 126*b*, 128*t*, 130*t*, 132*t*, 132*b*, 133*t*, 133*b*, 134, 135, 137, 138*t*; Alan Smith: pp. 2, 15, 55*br*, 59*b*, 61*t*, 63*tl*, 67*tr*, 106*b*, 107*t*, 107*b*, 110*t*, 110*b*, 114*b*, 118*b*, 125, 140, 143*r*; Sandy Tudhope: pp. 5, 10*t*, 103*t*; Members of the 1978/9 Chagos Expedition: pp. 36, 51, 62*b*, 82*b*, 99, 145.

FOREWORD

I first made my acquaintance with a real live coral reef as leader of Phase 6 of the Royal Society's expedition to Aldabra in the Indian Ocean when the task of my party was to survey the reef front and to attempt an inventory of its diversity. After my first reef dive, I could not help thinking that we were faced with an impossible task. Yet it soon became obvious that, within the teeming jumble of life, there was a certain uniformity of arrangement, a sense of pattern, which in time began to appear.

It was two expeditions later that I had the pleasure of working with the author of this book to further probe these patterns and relationships. The location was again the Indian Ocean, to be exact the Chagos Bank which forms its living centre. Our aim was much the same, to survey and map the coral communities of this giant submerged atoll. We were part of the Joint Services Expedition to Danger Island and, with the back-up expertise of divers and technicians from the Army, Navy and Air Force, we were able to spend more time amongst the world of the living reef and to ask and answer more exacting questions.

Charles Sheppard has gone on to continue this work in other locations in the Indian Ocean and,

more recently, on the Great Barrier Reef itself. His work, and that of many others, is at last allowing us to understand the true dynamics of reef formation and the communities which make them possible, the zones and zone boundaries determined by competition for space and resources and mediated by complex antibioses, and the constant struggle for dominance which hones each species to the perfection of a job well done in the community of life.

I will not spoil the book by revealing any more. Coral reefs are one of the great wonders of the world and the more you learn about them the more wonderful and awe-inspiring they become. Now, thanks to the development of the Self-Contained Underwater Breathing Apparatus and the training and technology that goes with it, the ultimate experience—a trip into a completely natural environment, a dive onto a pristine reef—is within the compass of millions. If you read this book before you dive, the experience will be even more worthwhile for it is written by a scientist, a diver and, above and below all, a conservationist. If you go, cause as little disturbance as you can; collect nothing, take only photographs, learn from your visit and leave the experience behind for others to enjoy.

David Bellamy

To Anne

PRELUDE

A CORAL REEF brings different images to the minds of different people. To a sea captain they are awesome structures, often poorly marked upon his chart and always at just the depth most likely to cause trouble. To the native of the tropics they are a home. The abundant fish support his family and he builds a house upon the coral islands. To the diver they are inspiring, a colourful wonderland of nature which he can watch and photograph at leisure. As for the scientist, he sees something more again, a place of seeming chaos in which he tries to find some order, some patterns and some clues to how it works.

For everyone, reefs are daunting places. They support more kinds of life than any other area in the sea and they themselves are built by that life. Here, like no other place, different branches of science tend to merge. What are you to make of an animal or a plant which makes rock? Is it a problem for biology or geology? Making rock is exactly what several forms of reef life do, particularly the corals.

There are several different kinds of reefs. The sort that people mostly live on are called *atolls*. From the depths of the Indian and Pacific Oceans rise hundreds of curious, conical mountains, rising a kilometre or more from the sea bed and ending at just about sea level. Living reefs cap the tops of them, extending down only to about a hundred metres where the sunlight reaches. The living reef does not extend above the water level, but low-lying islands edge above the surface, never more than a few metres high. These may be covered with rich vegetation and they are home to several animal species, especially birds, and support the villages of man himself.

The islands and adjacent shallow reefs of atolls form rings of colourful coral which show up brightly against the deep blue of the sea. The rings enclose lagoons of water which are shallow compared to the ocean outside, and look more emerald from the air. The circles are not complete and breaks allow free movement of water between the lagoon and open ocean. The panoramic view from an aircraft shows that the rings usually exist in groups and within each group there may be both large and small rings, round and oval ones, and others which are far from circular. A group is generally called an *archipelago* by geographers.

Towards the continents of the tropical oceans lie other kinds of reef. On the continental shelf of eastern Australia is the largest series of coral structures of all, the Great Barrier Reef. Here too are a few circles of coral reef, but they are not strictly atolls and, in addition, there is a great variety of other shapes and sizes as well, making up this barrier which stretches for over 1600 kilometres. These reefs, like some others near to continents, rise from a relatively shallow, silted plain only a few tens or hundreds of metres deep instead of the kilometres of their mid-oceanic counterparts. These patches and long unbroken ribbons may be out of sight of land, but they are still influenced by the continent and its shelf.

Barrier reefs are found in the Indian, Pacific and

The curve of an atoll rim is marked by a chain of palm-covered coral islands and by breakers curling onto the shallow reef flat to seaward of the islands. To the right of these, the reef slopes downwards for thousands of metres. To the left of the islands is a shallow lagoon.

can see below the surface in a number of ways, such as watching from a glass-bottomed boat or with a mask and snorkel. The way which gives the most freedom though is by using the kind of diving apparatus whereby you take your air down with you. Then, on a single dive, you may see a hundred different kinds and shapes of coral, a thousand types of fish and countless other animals and plants. Depending on the area, the numbers and the types will differ, but all reefs teem with life and colour.

To many, reefs are the most intriguing ecosystems that have ever appeared in the World's oceans. In some ways they are robust, but in others they are very fragile. Their complexity is such that they are visual chaos, but the work of the biologist, ever since he began to study coral reefs, has been to find the order that must lie within; to find the patterns and explain them. This is necessary because, taken as a part of the whole pattern of research, it provides better insights into how nature organises itself, how we interact with it, how we have harmed it and, then, how we can live within it with a minimum of disruptive impact. As part of this, many branches of marine science have developed, involving researchers with either a narrow focus onto a key component or a broader view. Their discoveries form the basis of this book, which tells how the reef lives and grows. Above all, we see how it *works*, what makes it the richest oasis of life that has ever been and why it is that, for all the vast number of different animals and plants which live there, it is one single, highly-integrated entity. We will not be looking at each of the major groups of life in turn and describing them, even though each group deserves to have its own separate story told. The story instead is of how they all mesh together in one vast web of life. Of course, as the reef is made of these species, they are still the stars of the story. But none on the reef can live in isolation and it is the processes of life and of living which are the main themes. It is often impossible also, to distinguish between the life and the geology of a reef since one makes the other and the other supports the first in an enormous wheel, driven, as all Earth's systems are, by the sun and affected by the wind and waves. This book is, in short, a story of the nature of the reef: a natural history.

Atlantic Oceans, though many are relatively small. Also found throughout the tropics is another kind of reef, one which is always seen even more closely adjoining land. This is a *fringing reef* and it may circle a small, mountainous island or it may border a part of a continent. The reef may continue unbroken until, perhaps, a river mouth forces a passage through the otherwise continuous fringe of surf and shallow water just offshore. These reefs follow the curves and turns of land, widening in places and shrinking in others, with many departures further out, giving rise to many isolated patches and complex shoals where corals grow.

From above the surface of the water, the variety of shapes which a coral reef can form seems endless and, indeed, it is. Underlying this variety, however, are some patterns and principles which serve to show us how this enormous range of shapes comes from a much smaller number of themes. Finding these is one of the purposes of reef science.

If, from the surface, the variety of shapes and sizes of reef seems endless, then below the surface the confusion and profusion of life is overwhelming. You

Looking to seaward on a coral island. The water is only waist-deep right out to the line of breakers, then it slopes downwards. Old coral rock forms this island, whose edge has a few self-seeded palms and shrubs.

The three-dimensional freedom of SCUBA diving is the best way to see the reef. This reef slope is packed with coral.

1. A SEA OF CORAL

THERE ARE two dotted lines on most maps of the World, lying about 23° North and South of the Equator. They mark the positions where the sun shines directly overhead in the midsummer of each hemisphere, and are called the Tropics of Capricorn and Cancer. Between them, the sun passes overhead twice each year, heating the land and surface layers of the oceans. In this area are most of the corals and coral reefs of the World.

The spread of coral reefs over the oceans is not just a matter of being in the tropics, however. Where there are warm currents leaving the region, such as those that flow towards Bermuda from the Carib-

bean and towards Japan from the China Sea, there the reefs go also. Where cold currents sweep into the region, as they do on the west coast of Africa, for example, there the corals will be few and the reefs will be small or even non-existent. In other words, reefs are features of warm water.

Coral reefs are structures which are built by a number of complex events, but their most basic component and that which provides most of the rock is the coral itself. Reef-building corals are colonies of simple animals which, in their countless billions, lay down millions of tonnes of rock. All forms of life have their preferred temperature ranges and these lowly

The key to the coral reefs of the world is the coral colony. They contain hundreds or thousands of tiny, tentacled animals which together build a strong skeleton of stone. Many different shapes and kinds exist. Countless stony skeletons over countless years build coral reefs. This is a species from the most numerous and widespread group of all—*Acropora*.

but vital creatures are no exception. Their choice is warm water and they can grow to build reefs only between sea-water temperatures of about 18 to 30°C. Where the seasonal water temperatures do not fluctuate too greatly beyond these limits, there the potential exists for reef-building corals to grow.

Patterns of Coral Reefs

The pattern of coral reef distribution therefore roughly follows that of warm sea water. Roughly that is, but not exactly. The first thing that causes exceptions is the distribution of suitable substrate for corals to grow on. The sorts of corals which build reefs need light in order to grow and build their skeletons and cannot just grow upward from any depth. Only shallow water will do. So, where the oceans have no shallow platforms, coral reefs will not be found even if the temperatures are right.

The result of this is clear from Figure 1. In all three oceans which have tropical areas, the Atlantic, the Indian and Pacific, coral reefs are concentrated towards their western ends. The Caribbean and its multitude of islands, coral keys and fringing reefs is in the west of the Atlantic; the majority of the reefs and atolls of the Indian Ocean lie between the central line and the African coast; while in the Pacific also it is the central to western part which contains most of the South Sea islands, coral reefs and atolls. The reason in all cases is that these areas have most of the platforms, volcanic and other geological structures which have produced islands and shallow areas. The mass of islands in the area which divides the Indian and Pacific Oceans has the largest amount of shoreline and shallow water of all, however, and so has a correspondingly rich and extensive collection of reefs. These are all the results of enormous, ancient and continuing earth movements and complex geological conditions and they have greatly affected the positions of the World's reefs.

The second thing which interferes with the growth of corals and coral reefs is the quality of the sea water. Corals are very intolerant of fresh water and of a lot of silt in the water. They do not survive at all, for example, where rivers pour into the sea. This excludes them from a lot of places, even where the water is warm and there is suitable substrate. Breaks in fringing reefs opposite river mouths are proof of this and many cities and towns owe their positions to the safe passage that this gives to ships. Even the massive Great Barrier Reef is turned and stopped at its northern end by the torrents coming from Papua New Guinea, and the River Amazon in South America also prevents the Caribbean reefs from extending southwards along the coast of that continent.

The reef surrounding much of this Pacific island is cut through by a small river. The channel leading to the shore is over 40 metres deep; quite safe for boats. The channel occurs because reef-building organisms cannot grow in the freshwater outflow.

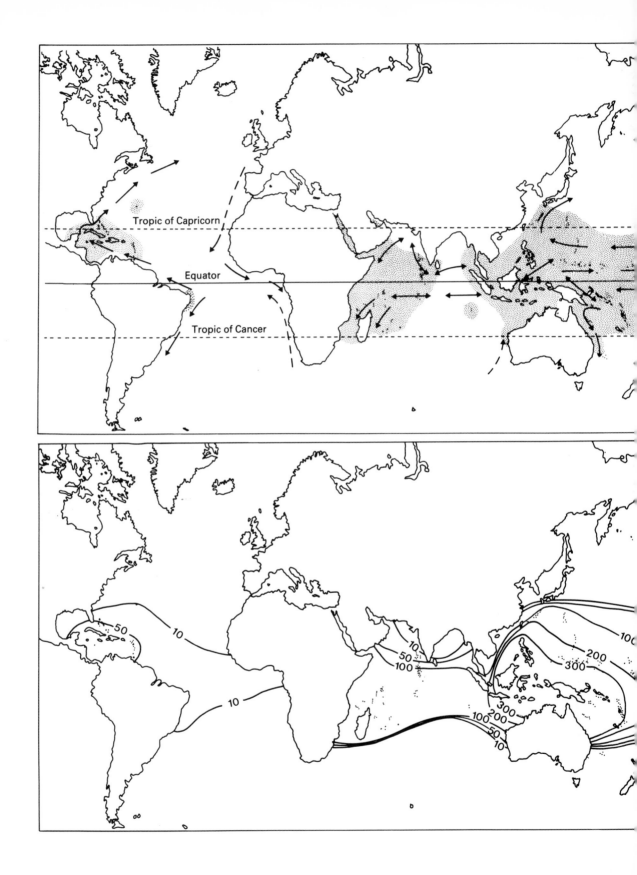

Tropic of Capricorn

Equator

Tropic of Cancer

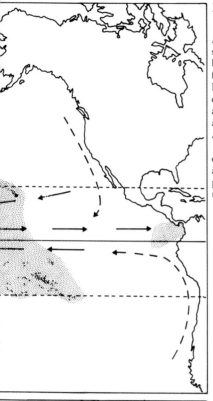

Fig. 1. These two maps should be looked at together. The first concerns coral reefs and the second concerns the corals which build them. Generally the coral reefs of the world lie between the Tropics of Capricorn and Cancer. Exceptions to this occur where warm water flows out of this area. In the Caribbean, the Gulf Stream supports coral reefs in Florida and Bermuda. In the Indo-Pacific, reefs extend to Japan and along the Hawaiian chain, and the coral-rich Great Barrier Reef of Australia extends well beyond the Tropic. Warm currents are shown as unbroken arrows. Cold currents, which inhibit reefs, are shown as dashed arrows and are the reason why reefs are absent, for example, in west Africa and most of west America. Shaded areas mark the general areas where coral reefs grow.

Within the tropics, no reefs are found where conditions are unsuitable, even though some corals may grow. The northern Indian Ocean's shores, the northern Persian Gulf and the area around Hong Kong, for example, are all too muddy, too hot or flushed with rivers to permit significant reef growth. In the tropical oceans, the western parts support more reefs than the eastern parts because the vast majority of islands and shallow areas exist there.

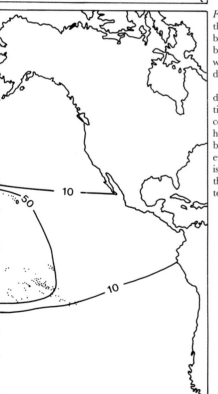

Fig. 2. The contour lines show the approximate numbers of species of reef-building corals that exist in the oceans. Many reef-building corals can be found growing on rocky substrates beyond the limits of reef growth shown in the first map, even though they can no longer build reefs. In west Africa, for example, several species grow, and Indo-Pacific corals extend well south of the Great Barrier Reef, penetrating deep into the kelp forests before disappearing.

The Caribbean is the richest Atlantic area, with approximately seventy-five species. In decreasing numbers, they spread down to Brazil and Africa. The Indo-Pacific is several times richer and here also the number of species declines unevenly as distance from the central focus increases. In this vast area, some spread across almost the whole region. Others have more limited ranges, many being confined to the highest diversity area, but others being found only in restricted parts of the Indian Ocean. Very substantial fringing reefs and even atolls in the Pacific are built by a mere fifty species or less and, down to this level, there is no clear connection between the numbers of different coral species which build a reef and the substantiveness or size of the reef. Below about fifty species in the Indo-Pacific, reefs do tend to become smaller and less developed.

Some coral species occur over huge areas, *Pocillopora eydouxi* (*top*) is one which occurs over most of the Indo-Pacific. Many others live in relatively small areas: *Turbinaria heronensis* (*above*) has been found only on the Great Barrier Reef within the rich area shown in the previous map. The reasons why some species are widespread and common while others are restricted and rare is not known at present.

The requirements of corals are therefore very strict. It is perhaps surprising that there are so many areas which do fulfil their demands except that, to a large extent, corals provide their own areas on which to live. Their process of growth means that they have made, and are still making, their own substrate in shallow seas away from fresh and turbid water.

We can see, therefore, that there is a pattern to the distribution of coral reefs which goes beyond merely being tropical. The species of corals which live on them also have a pattern.

Patterns of Corals

The second map (Fig. 2) shows the second broad pattern, not of where reefs are, but of where most reef-building coral species are and how many may be found at each location. It shows contour lines enclosing numbers of species, which radiate out from two central points. It shows clearly that, in the Atlantic Ocean, the Caribbean is the centre of the coral world and that most species in this Ocean are found there. The richness of coral species, or *diversity* as it is called, falls off as distance from the central Caribbean increases.

The contour picture is similar and even more marked in the much larger Indian and Pacific Oceans. These two oceans are closely connected through the warm waters which lie between South-East Asia and Australia. As far as the corals and other marine life are concerned, these two oceans are one and the term 'Indo-Pacific Ocean' is given to describe this enormous but biologically continuous body of water. In the Indo-Pacific, the richest area for coral species is centred on the Philippine to north Australian regions. But, as in the Caribbean, as the distance from there increases, the number of coral species falls rapidly. This happens even though the sea temperature remains suitable and the substrate is stable and shallow. The reasons for the fall-off in each case are not really known, although several theories have been put forward to explain it. These suggest that colder water temperatures in the fairly recent past, rates of coral dispersal, or even different rates of coral evolution in different areas, may be responsible.

Something else which is evident from this map is that the number of species in the Atlantic, even at its richest point in the central Caribbean, is much lower than in the central Indo-Pacific. Only about seventy-five species exist in the Caribbean and its outlying areas, compared to four or five hundred in the Indo-Pacific. What is also the case is that the types or species of coral in each area are quite different.

It seems that there are no species which are common to both regions. At the level of genus, however, which is the next level of classification (see p. 28) there are a few which are common to the two regions. These include the two genera, *Acropora* and *Porites*, which are abundant and important reef-builders on both Atlantic and Indo-Pacific reefs. At even higher levels of classification, such as that of family, the two regions hold much in common.

Because no species are common to both regions, the world has two different sets of corals, one in the Atlantic and one in the Indo-Pacific. However, from the fact that genera and families of corals become increasingly common to both regions, it is deduced that both groups have a common ancestry, and this is supported by evidence from the fossil records. What happened was that long ago the two regions were joined by a warm water link; they were part of the same ocean in fact. Then the continents moved. The Atlantic became separated from the Indian Ocean by movements of Africa, and it became separated from the Pacific when the Isthmus of Panama rose up. The Atlantic was isolated as far as warm-water corals were concerned. Although water flows freely around the southern tips of Africa and America, such waters are too cold for corals. They cannot grow and their larvae die, so it is as effective a barrier as dry land. Then, over a period of time, evolution proceeded apace. Each group evolved in its own way and each produced the different species which have today resulted in the two great coral regions of the world.

Making a Coral Reef

When corals make reefs, they build in a very wide range of shapes and sizes. However, within this variety lie several basic shapes and patterns which allow reefs to be grouped into just a few categories. How the atolls and banks of coral which lie scattered over the Indo-Pacific and Atlantic Oceans were formed has been a topic of discussion in reef science for many years.

Several theories have been proposed concerning

Although coral species from the Atlantic and Indo-Pacific are completely different, members from both regions which live in similar zones of their respective reefs, often look and behave alike. These deep-water corals, *Leptoseris*, from the Indo-Pacific (*top*) and *Agaricia* from the Atlantic (*above*) both have similar, leafy growths. Similar correspondences occur in most types, including branched and brain corals. Often the look-alike corals from the two regions are related, dating from when the two regions were connected about fifty million years ago.

how reefs are made and they have tried to address one or both of two related but separate problems: how the platforms on which the reefs lie arose and what has caused the present shape of the reefs. Several theories supplement each other, while others are contradictory. Features of a number of theories have still been retained, while others have been

9

(*Above*) A fringing reef around an old volcanic island is the first stage in the development of many reefs. The darker strip just landward of the breakers is rock, living corals and algae. The lighter-coloured strip to landward is a slightly deeper, sandy area. The seaward edge of this reef plummets steeply.

(*Left*) Part of a barrier reef, this structure lies on the edge of the continental shelf off Australia over a hundred kilometres from land. Between the land and the reef the sea is only one or two hundred metres deep, but immediately to seaward of the reef the terrain drops steeply to depths of thousands of metres.

(*Above*) Coral atolls are rings of reef and islands found mostly in mid-ocean. The lagoons enclosed by the rings are relatively shallow, although the water around the outside of the atoll may be several kilometres deep. This atoll is fairly small so the islands on the opposite side of its lagoon can be seen.

(*Left*) A fringe of coral so thin it is scarcely a reef. This Caribbean coral community has all the profusion and diversity of life contained on any reef but it is little more than a veneer on the side of a volcano which rises from deep water. You only need to drill a very short distance inwards to reach volcanic rock as there is not the great thickness of limestone which a well-established coral reef would have. Under water, however, it looks like a reef and is probably growing outwards very slowly.

discarded or are thought to have a very limited application.

It was Charles Darwin who came up with an elegant solution of how atolls might be formed. In his voyage around the World, he had seen fossilised marine species at high altitudes in the Andes Mountains and realised that parts of the Earth's crust must move vertically over considerable distances. At that time, the possibility that parts of the Earth could move was nearly as controversial as his later theory of evolution proved to be. His theory of atoll formation was based on two main factors: a gradual subsidence of the platform on which corals grew and the assumption that corals, and the reefs which they built, could grow upwards at least as fast. The theory has withstood most of the tests of 150 years of further research and it also explains the formation not only of atolls but of two other reef types as well. These, the fringing and barrier reefs, are all linked together in a simple progression.

Initially a volcano, protruding from the warm, coral sea, develops a fringe of coral around it in shallow water—a fringing reef. The volcano slowly subsides into the sea and, while it does so, the upward growth of the coral maintains the position of the reef in shallow water. If it grows up and outwards all the time, at a later stage, a channel may develop between the reef and the island. When this reaches a certain stage it is called a barrier reef. (Clearly there is a lot of flexibility over the point at which one becomes the other; one long-standing suggestion is that when the channel has become big enough to take a large boat the reef is a barrier reef.) Very large numbers of fringing reefs and barrier reefs exist around the world.

Eventually the volcano will become submerged and be lost to sight, leaving only the ring of coral. This is now an atoll. Many hundreds of atolls exist in the Indian and Pacific Oceans, ranging in size from about 1 to over 160 kilometres in diameter, but mostly about 3 to 30 kilometres across. Darwin's scheme predicts very well how it is that so many atolls can exist and it replaced an earlier idea that atolls were formed by reefs growing around the rims of extinct and submerged volcano craters. A growth around a rim of a volcano which was at a suitable depth could happen, but there was no way of explaining how so many volcano rims happened to be at the same depth.

All three stages and many intermediate ones can be seen in the coral seas today. Holes which have been drilled deep into the reef have confirmed that the coral rock does indeed often sit on top of older volcanic rock. Fossils of terrestrial animals and shallow water species have been brought up from the bottom of these drill cores, proving that no matter how deep they are today, they were once at sea level or above. Radio-isotope dating has given ages for how long the whole process has taken in some cases, and these range from a few thousands to many millions of years.

Many reefs, however, resisted such a simple explanation as that of Darwin. The Great Barrier Reef, for example, is not just a large-scale version of this process. In fact, it is not a single barrier reef at all, but a huge complex of many quite different shapes, sizes and types of reef which lie on the continental shelf in water which is very shallow compared to that of their mid-oceanic counterparts.

Later additions to the theory occurred when it became clear that the sea level had changed considerably in relation to the land. Ice Ages have come and gone, periodically withdrawing and releasing large volumes of water which have resulted in the alternate emergence and drowning of the reefs and, added to this, there have been vertical movements of the land itself. So the present shallow areas where reefs grow have not always been shallow, or even wet, which complicates the ideas of how reefs grow.

Following these important discoveries, an American called Daly developed a theory of 'glacial control' of reef building in the early part of this century. At first, some regarded this as a contradiction of Darwin's theory, but in fact Darwin explained how reefs originated and Daly explained how sea-level changes and erosion could cause surface features. He thought that when sea level fell and water temperature fell in an Ice Age, corals could not protect the reefs. Then, reefs, and even volcanoes, might be planed down by waves. When the water rose again, corals had a suitable platform and would, for ecological reasons, grow most vigorously around the edge.

For various reasons, including the fact that erosion is slower than Daly thought, this is now largely discounted, although Daly did show that no theory can now ignore sea-level changes or erosion by sea and rain.

It was once suggested that the disk shape of an atoll might be caused by the solution by sea water of the rock in the centre of a flat planed reef. This theory, however, was abandoned when it was realised that sea water could not dissolve coral rock at the necessary rate. A newer theory suggests that, instead, acid rain dissolves out the disk shapes when the reefs are exposed in times of low sea level and this is regarded as being more plausible.

It is clear that many factors are involved in the making of a coral reef and this means that ideas of the ways in which reefs are formed are now very much more complicated than was envisaged a century ago. We now know quite a lot about many of the underlying principles, although a lot more research is still needed to make the picture clearer.

A Medium for Growth

Whatever the details of the mechanisms of reef formation, another important consideration is the chemistry of the water which bathes them. In most cases, the open oceans which surround reefs show a much lower diversity and abundance of life than the reef does. This is because, although the tropical oceans are rich in many of the chemicals which are essential for life, they are quite poor in some others which limits the life that can be supported in them. As a result, the waters which flow onto a reef from the open ocean have low densities of plankton and larger forms of life. Against this background of sparse ocean life, the coral reef stands out in dramatic contrast, like a tumultuous oasis of life in a relatively barren watery desert.

As the reef is a living system, it needs a certain quantity of nutrients and minerals to keep it going. Those which are abundant in the water which flows past are removed from the water in the quantities which are needed. Those which are not abundant are also removed, stored and used. Of these, the reef may receive only a tiny trickle from outside, but it

traps and stores them with great efficiency. It permits only a negligible amount to leak away once it has been trapped and it continually recycles what it has, so that, although it may not be considered rich in these substances, it clearly has built up considerable reserves of them. These reserves are locked up in the structure of the reef and within its numerous forms of life.

Calcium carbonate is the substance which corals and other animals and plants deposit and there is plenty of this mineral available. The sea around the coral reef is saturated with it and organisms extract it from the water to deposit it in their skeletons. A certain amount continually redissolves back into the water, so that a cycle exists of this mineral, which is the foundation of the reef itself.

The basis of the organic life of the reef is the material made by the plants, just as it is in all other living systems. The plants make carbohydrates and other compounds by combining carbon with hydrogen into complex molecules by the process of photosynthesis. The carbon for this comes from the water's plentiful dissolved load of calcium carbonate. There is an infinite amount also of that other part of the carbohydrate molecule: hydrogen. The plants obtain this element by splitting water molecules, which are a combination of hydrogen and oxygen, releasing the oxygen and binding the hydrogen onto the carbon. For these major elements which make up the living tissue, therefore, there is no shortage of raw materials. There is also an inexhaustible supply of oxygen dissolved in the water, coming from the atmosphere and from the plants' photosynthesis. By themselves, however, these elements cannot form all higher compounds and cannot support life. Other elements are needed. Some are required in still substantial amounts, such as nitrogen and phosphorus, while many trace elements, which provide minute but vital parts of many chemical mechanisms in all living things, are also needed and must be found.

Nitrogen is a special case. There are some primitive organisms the world over which can take in nitrogen from the atmosphere (or from solution in water) and turn it into more complex and biologically useful compounds. Two groups of organisms can do this; bacteria and some of a group of plants

The coral reef is a focus and a substrate for more forms of life than are found anywhere else in the sea. Corals, a vase sponge and a colony of hydroids take what minerals and nutrients they can from the water. Nutrients are scarce in the water which bathes a reef, but those locked up in the tissues of animals are recycled rapidly and efficiently.

called blue-green algae. These are small to microscopic in size but enormous in importance. They were around in the seas long before the higher organisms for which they paved the way. They exist on the reef in films covering rock and sand and commonly in symbiotic association with larger organisms, such as sponges. They also thrive in beds of sea grasses where these are present. In all these places, they grow and form nitrogenous compounds of kinds which can be used by all the other sorts of life on the reef. These primitive organisms thus play an essential role in the metabolism of the reef as a whole.

Phosphorus is another vital element needed by plants and animals. The supply of this to the reef is extremely low, but reefs have a supply locked up within their system. Firstly, there is a lot tied up in the living tissues of the organisms themselves. This becomes available to animals when they eat one another or graze on a plant. Another large sink of phosphorus, however, is the sediment. The element

binds on to the surfaces of rock, and the surface area of rock in just a bucket of sand and sediment is hundreds of square metres. Phosphorus sticks to this and exchanges fairly readily with water, so that, when sediment is disturbed, some phosphorus is released. It can return to this sink equally easily and does so, for example, from the bodies of those numerous organisms which live and die within the sand.

It is possibly true that there are shortages of some critical elements and these shortages slow down the life on the reef. There is a sufficiency of many ele-

The concentration of fish on a reef is greater than that in open water, partly because the reef provides shelter but also because it provides food. In turn, fish provide food for others and are important in nutrient-recycling. These fish are *Pempheris*.

ments, however, even if it is almost always locked away.

So coral reefs have developed living systems which tightly recycle everything and are near to being self-contained for what they need. They have a minimum of unused wastes because chemicals cycle from species to species as each consumes the other, with very little leaking out of and escaping from the living part of the reef. Physically and chemically the sea around a reef shapes it and supports all its forms of life.

Coral Reefs in Perspective

The reefs which dot the tropical seas are so extensive that the word 'reef' itself has become synonymous with 'coral reef'. Their dominance in the warm, well-lit sea, though, is a relatively recent event in geological time. From the beginning of multi-cellular life, many other types of reef made from organisms quite different from corals have existed and many were of comparable importance. The coral reef is only the latest in a long line and Figure 3 helps us to put coral reefs into perspective.

We see that reefs have developed on many occasions during the immensity of time that life has existed in our seas. The plants and animals which made them have been quite unrelated, except for a common ability to secrete deposits of durable rock, mostly calcium carbonate. Most have supported great diversities of other life forms and the results of their building have had enormous influence in the tropical seas of their day.

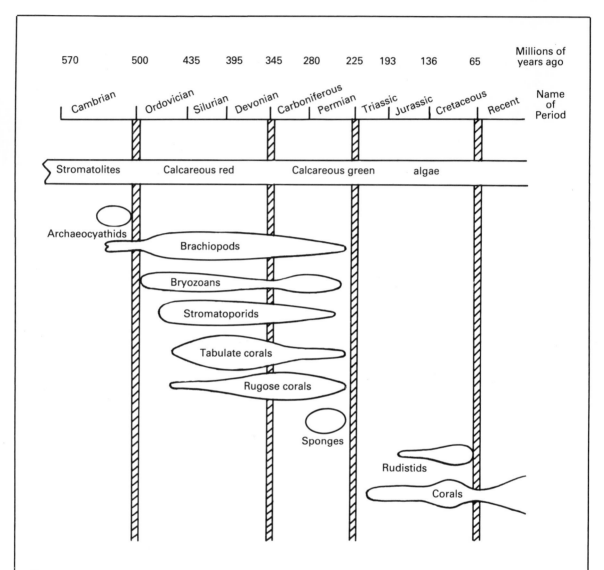

Fig. 3. Modern or stony corals have been building reefs for only a small part of the time for which life has existed. This diagram shows which organisms built reefs since the Cambrian period over half a billion years ago. Many of them are now extinct. Some, like brachiopods, bryozoans and sponges, are still very much around, although they no longer build reefs.

Algae were the first. They still construct a few reefs and they are a vital part of coral reefs too. From top to bottom, archaeocyathids were like sponges, while brachiopods were, and still are, shelled animals. Bryozoans are primitive colonial animals and the extinct stromatoporids were a kind of primitive sponge. Tabulate and rugose corals were coelenterates, like modern corals, and rudistids are an extinct group of giant bivalve molluscs. These are now mostly seen scattered over the continents and in mountain ranges a long way from the sea as a result of upheavals of the Earth's crust.

All reefs supported rich communities of other forms of life, just as modern coral reefs do, some components of which added quite substantially to the limestone. Four times over this immense period, large amounts of the World's species have been swept away by unknown forces, the biggest collapse being at the end of the Permian period. In Recent times, corals and algae are seen as the main reef builders but, as we see in this book, many other types of animal life are important to the process of reef building.

The passing of the different forms of reefs reflects the impermanence, on a geological scale, of the different forms of life. Several worldwide crashes have occurred which have seen the end of numerous forms of life, including several reef-builders. The reasons for these tremendous waves of extinctions are still not understood.

There is no reason to assume that the life and reefs of today are any more secure. Evidence is increasing which shows that species are becoming extinct more frequently today than they did in any past collapse, including the one that swept away the dinosaurs. This time, however, man is to blame. Some reef systems are becoming dangerously imperilled by disturbance, collecting or pollution. In numerous instances, reefs have been reported to be damaged and sections sometimes dying. Of an entire reef, whose foundations are several kilometres thick, only a thin skin is made of living organisms. We must not assume that they are here to stay or that we cannot easily eliminate them.

The structures built up by corals over millions of years can be immense. They are the largest construc-

tions on Earth and it is said that the Great Barrier Reef can even be seen from the moon. For most of us, the presence of a reef is simply detected by a change in the colour of the sea from the blue of deep water to the turquoise and emeralds of the shallows and by a line of white surf. Except at extreme low tides, the coral-covered reef never reaches above the level of the water; it is a product of the sea.

The reef is shaped to a large degree by its interaction with the sea, but it is also shaped by the life processes of the reef itself. Despite the wide range of shapes that reefs have when viewed from above, a smaller slice through each shows us that there are many similarities in all of them and that their similarities are greater than their differences. The life of a reef shows an exceptional degree of interdependence and its processes are in dynamic equilibrium. But over periods of time, growth has generally exceeded loss to result in the present-day reefs of the World. In a sense, the corals and other organisms which build the reefs are living rocks and it is on them, and on the plants and animals that live with them, that the richest areas of life in the tropical seas depend.

This coral reef in the middle of a field was growing beneath the sea about 290 000 years ago. Past movements of the land and of the sea levels mean that old reefs of many types are now high and dry.

(*Left*) This shallow scene shows four or five species of branching and plate corals which all belong to one single group (or genus) called *Acropora*. This is the largest group of stony, or true, corals and contains nearly a hundred species altogether—about one-fifth of all reef-building corals.

Part of a colony of a branching *Acropora* in close-up. Numerous tiny polyps with short tentacles are set in cups around each branch. Each cup houses one polyp and very thin connecting tissue covers all the rest of the surface as well. Both the polyps and the tissue joining them together deposit limestone in a shape characteristic of the coral species. There is a larger cup at the tip of each branch which shows the place and direction of growth.

The largest coral colonies of all are those of the Caribbean elk-horn, *Acropora palmata*, a thickly branched species from shallow water.

Polyps of the genus *Goniopora* are extended day and night except when touched. Long, cylindrical polyp stalks are filled with water. Each is crowned with a ring of tentacles which surrounds the mouth. These polyps are 5 millimetres across and are exceptionally long for corals, reaching about 10 centimetres or more in length.

2. ANIMAL ARCHITECTS

A DIVER seeing his first coral reef may be visually overwhelmed. Hundreds of colours, thousands of species and an infinity of shapes and sizes are present. Stag's-horns and thickets tower above many smaller forms. In the Caribbean, flexible, branching gorgonians crowd onto the substrate, while on Indo-Pacific reefs soft corals jostle with hard corals for space. Tremendous activity is added by the fish, singly, in pairs or in schools, feeding on the bottom-living life or on each other. Then, many other life forms become apparent—starfish, molluscs and crustaceans. In fact, more major categories of life occur in this relatively small area than anywhere else on land or sea.

It might at first be difficult to focus down onto specific things. Although, as we shall see, all the groups of animals here have a firm place and an important role to play in the scheme of things, one particular group is of great and immediate importance. It is to this that we must first look to find an understanding of the life of the reef and of how the reef itself is made.

This group is the coelenterates. They cover the rocky substrate, occupying anything from at least three-quarters of it to often the whole of it. This group includes the corals, soft corals, sea fans, hydroids and many other less conspicuous forms as well. Another form, the sea anemone, is possibly the living ancestor of all the other attached forms. All play a role in the pattern of life, but none more so than the corals. So it is possible to see what a coelenterate is and how it works by looking at a typical coral.

Anatomy of a Reef-builder

A single coral animal is a polyp. It resembles closely the anemone to which it is related. It has one or more rings of tentacles surrounding a mouth, leading to the main body cavity in a stalk which is able to contract. On the tentacles are small stinging darts, called *nematocysts*, with which it captures prey, for all corals are carnivores to some degree. The polyp may remain solitary in a few species, but in most corals the initial polyp buds off others, forming colonies of thousands, even millions, of polyps. Each of them stays connected to its neighbours by living tissue.

This is simple enough, and corals would be fairly unremarkable if it were not for an ability which lifts them to great importance: the polyps and the tissues connecting them can secrete limestone rock.

The simplicity of this definition, however, hides one of the largest ranges of patterns, shapes and structures in the sea. The structure of one polyp may be simple, but the colony formations ramify into large boulders and tables and into exquisite shapes of the most complex sort, governed by the genes of the particular species of polyp and by the conditions and turbulence of the sea. In uncountable numbers, these small animals will grow, laying down rock by the millions of tonnes, forming reefs and forming their own substrate.

Fig. 4. Simplified family tree of the coelenterates. Corals (*1*) are close relatives of zoanthids (*2*), which are polyps without a limestone skeleton, and of sea anemones (*3*). This group is related to the octocorals, which include the soft corals (*4*) and sea fans (*5*), and to a group called *Telestacea* (*6*), which bears a resemblance to both. (*7*) shows typical polyps of all the octocorals and represents other groups, such as the stony false corals; blue coral and the red organ-pipe coral. Precious black corals or antipatharians (*8*) form an offshoot from this main right-hand stem of Anthozoa. Less closely-related coelenterates on the left-hand stem are the Medusozoa, which include the true jellyfish (*9*), siphonophores such as the Portugese-man-of-war (*10*), hydroids (*11*) and the stony fire coral *Millepora* (*12*). Relationships are worked out not by the very variable overall shapes but by detailed inspection of the animals' anatomy.

(*Right*) The polyps of most stony corals are tiny yet build enormous limestone structures. Common shapes are boulders and the surface of each boulder-forming coral has a different pattern sculpted on it. The boulder from which the scientist is chipping a sample has a wavy pattern; it is one of the Indo-Pacific brain corals called *Platygyra*.

A few reef-building coral species do not bud but remain as a single polyp. This large polyped *Cynarina lacrymalis* is 5 centimetres in diameter. Like most species, its tentacles are firmly retracted into the stony cup in daytime but, because its tissues are transparent, the white radial plates, or *septa*, can be seen beneath. The oval mouth is also partially open in the centre.

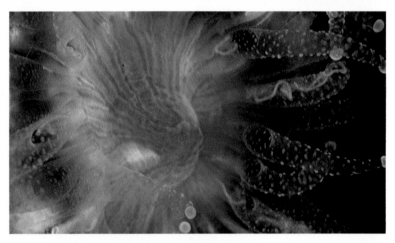

One magnified polyp from a stony coral of the group *Favia*. These polyps emerge only at night to catch zooplankton. On the transparent tentacles can be seen opaque spots: these are the batteries of stinging cells.

The second largest coral genus is *Porites*. Most of its species are shaped like small boulders. Others are leafy, while some are branching. This is a branching Indo-Pacific species and others of similar shape are of importance in shallow waters of Atlantic reefs.

(*Right*) Close up of the Indo-Pacific brain coral *Platygyra*. The tightly-contracted, pale green tissue of the polyps lies along the bottom of the valleys and cups. The walls between the polyps are also covered with a thin, brown layer of tissue.

(*Far right*) Soft corals come in many forms and they too are colonies of small polyps. The most obvious difference is that their skeletons are made of soft organic material, not rock, and the polyps always have eight tentacles instead of the six or multiples of six of the stony corals. This one is *Telesto*.

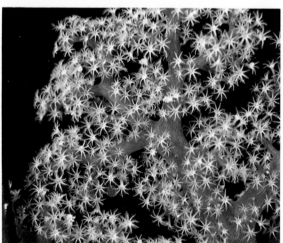

The coral polyp can be male or female, both or neither, and its reproductive organs are contained inside the body cavity. Its tissue is made up of two layers of cells. The outer one, the *ectoderm*, encloses it all. On the underside of the polyp, this layer contains the structures that deposit limestone. On the upper surface and on the tentacles, it contains the stinging cells. The ectoderm is separated from the inner layer, or *endoderm*, by the *mesoglea*, a jelly-like substance containing cell nuclei but not made of discrete cells in the same way. The endoderm lines the body cavity and forms digestive and reproductive structures. This layer is also found inside the tentacles and within the tissue which connects the polyps of a colony.

These layers are found in all coelenterates with small differences in the proportion and shape of each. They exist in a sea anemone and in a coral polyp and occur also in a jellyfish, which is another coelenterate, but an upside-down version compared to the others, with a vastly increased middle, or jelly, layer. These layers are characteristic of this very diverse and primitive group of animals.

The hard corals deposit limestone around and beneath each polyp and beneath the tissue which connects them all together in a colony. This is a result of the metabolism of the animal's tissue. The water which bathes each polyp is saturated in calcium carbonate, but the chemical conditions inside the polyp are quite different to that of sea water and permit much less calcium carbonate to remain in solution. The result is that a lot of this chemical precipitates out. In many coelenterates, it is secreted into the water, but in corals and similar animals it is formed, in ways which are still far from well understood, into crystals of calcium carbonate. These are then secreted in a matrix beneath and around the polyp. The result is the stony coral skeleton. It is pure, white calcium carbonate, or limestone.

The shape of each coral is the result of the way the polyps and connecting tissues of each colony lay this material down. Cup-shaped depressions on the surface of each indicate the position of the polyps and between them is an intricate pattern of ridges, bumps, spikes and other sculptured shapes. Each species deposits its limestone in a specific way. World-wide there are over a thousand different

species and so there are over a thousand different sculpted patterns on the surfaces of corals.

The soft corals do things differently. Instead of depositing limestone crystals, they deposit a jelly-like matrix which is impregnated with spicules of stony material. The jelly-like substance causes these colonies to be flexible and even soft to the touch. The polyps of sea fans similarly deposit a flexible material like soft corals, as do sea whips which are long, slender and unbranched colonies often several metres long.

These groups have a lot in common. All are colonies of very small polyps which deposit a base on which they grow, but it is the differences in their biology which are important and which lead to the

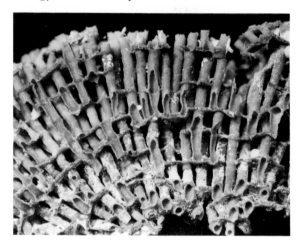

different shapes observed and to the different textures of each type of colony. One major difference is in the durability of their skeletons. When a coral colony dies it leaves behind a hard skeleton. This may remain more or less intact on the reef to provide some solid substrate, or, in the case of the delicate leafy and branching forms, the skeleton is usually rapidly broken up into fragments. Either way, the coral colony leaves a durable legacy which helps the reef to grow. When the soft corals and sea fans die, however, their soft, organic skeletons soon disintegrate without trace. The mass of tiny spicules embedded in the matrix is left, but this is only a tiny part. It is the rock-depositing polyps—the corals—that are crucial to the reef-building process. They are, therefore, to a large extent responsible for the continued existence of the other groups too. As we shall see later, there are many other facets to the building and maintainance of a reef in the face of violent erosional forces from the waves and from organisms which etch and weaken the rock, but many of the principal building blocks are those which are provided by the limestone-making corals.

Building Foundations

The amount of limestone deposited by the different species of coral varies enormously. Some corals grow extremely slowly, expanding their colonies by just a few millimetres each year. Others, particularly some branching corals, can expand by some 10 centimetres or more over the same time. It all depends on the growth pattern and nature of the species. The faster-growers, however, do not necessarily lay down a greater mass of rock. Because the diameter of a bushy species, for example, extends by 10 centimetres, it does not mean that more limestone has been deposited if its branches are thin or widely spaced. Furthermore, the texture of the deposited rock also varies greatly. Some corals lay down very light and porous skeletons, none more so than the well-named *Alveopora*, whose skeleton contains so much space that it floats when dry. Others deposit a solidly-packed skeleton which is very much more dense. *Leptastrea* is the most solid and contains almost no gaps or pores within its substance.

(*Top left*) A common soft coral called *Scleronephthya*. The fleshy skeletons of these disintegrate when the colony dies and do not add to the stonework of the coral reef.

(*Above left*) The tufts of feathery structures are hydroids, coelenterates which are rather distantly related to corals but which still share a similar body structure.

(*Left*) Some hydrozoan groups have stony skeletons, even though they are not true corals. This is *Stylaster*, a cave-dwelling coelenterate which looks superficially like a sea fan but which has a hard skeleton. Such organisms are often referred to as 'false corals'.

(*Above*) The stony skeleton of *Tubipora musica* is red, a feature which shows that it is a false coral. It is in the octocoral group and this cross-sectional view shows why it earned the common name of organ-pipe coral.

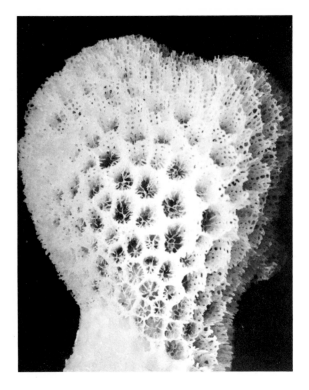

The Indo-Pacific coral *Alveopora* (*left*) has such a porous skeleton that it floats when dry. So will the lightest Atlantic coral called *Colpophyllia*, whose brain-like surface is shown in close-up (*right*).

A single polyp begins to make a skeleton as soon as it settles as a larva on the substrate. Some species of coral polyps remain solitary all their adult life and their skeleton remains fairly small. But the great skeleton-builders are the polyps which grow into colonies and it is to these that we usually refer when we speak of reef-building. Reef-building and the massive deposition of limestone that corals perform, can only occur because the initial polyps have the ability to multiply. They produce large numbers of exact copies of themselves which remain connected to each other and which all continuously deposit limestone. The corals' ability to bud is one of their most important characteristics.

Different methods of budding are seen. In the first, the circular ring of tentacles surrounding the mouth becomes oval and the mouth moves to one end. A second mouth develops within the ring of tentacles at the other end. This reflects also what is happening inside the body, where a division of the polyp is occurring. Then the oval tentacle ring constricts at a point between the two mouths and, when this is

complete, two polyps, each with its own ring of tentacles, are formed.

There are many variations on this theme. Often more than one secondary mouth will appear within the original ring of tentacles. There may be three in a triangle or three or more in linear array. Again the tentacle ring may constrict as before, resulting in three or more separate polyps. But in many types, only incomplete constriction occurs and the coral shows two adjacent polyps with only a partial separation. In several others, long lines of partially-budded polyps are formed in which numerous mouths appear in a very elongated ring of tentacles which shows no sign of constriction or completion of separation at all. The result in such cases is that long chains of closely-connected polyps form, meandering irregularly over the face of the adult colony.

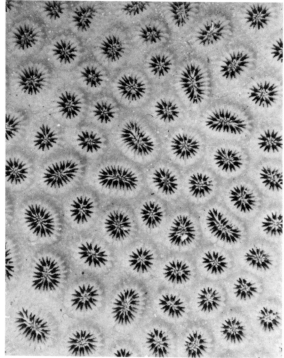

These are commonly termed 'brain corals'. You can choose whether to regard each elongated structure as one polyp with many partially-separated mouths or as many polyps which share a common ring of tentacles. It is all the same to the coral and it is a structure favoured by about a tenth of all reef-building species.

In these forms of budding, the second mouth appears within the original ring of tentacles. It is called therefore *intratentacular budding*. In a second form of budding, a new, or daughter, polyp grows from outside the tentacle ring of the parent, from the stalk perhaps or from the tissue which lies between the polyps. This form of budding, distinct from the previous form, is called *extratentacular budding*. This method will only ever produce single (or monocentric) and completely separate polyps, no matter how closely they may be touching. It cannot produce chains of polyps such as those of brain corals, where intratentacular budding is used.

In all cases, the deposition of the skeleton closely follows the deployment of a new polyp or of a part of one; thus the pattern on a coral skeleton, or *corallum*,

Surface of the Atlantic coral *Dichocoenia* (*left*) from which all tissue has been removed. Each round dish houses one polyp, but oval dishes develop when the polyp divides into two. This also occurs in the Indo-Pacific *Euphyllia* (*right*); in the foreground, one cup has nearly completed dividing into two. The principle is similar for both corals, only, in the first species, coral skeleton also fills in the space between the cups.

In this skeleton of the Atlantic brain coral, *Diploria*, the polyps kept on dividing but did not close off into single polyps as in the previous examples. The result is chains of still-fused polyps which lie in the valleys.

parallels instantly the position, the development and degree of separation of the new polyps.

Each coral species, and indeed each genus of corals, usually shows one form of budding and keeps to it always. (A genus is the level of grouping higher than species. It is a group name which precedes the species name when written. With *Acropora palifera*, for example, *palifera* designates the species, of which there are many in the genus *Acropora*. We can use *Acropora* on its own to denote the group of corals.) Most coral species bud in the extratentacular way, including the

largest coral colonies of all. In the Indo-Pacific, these are the branching colonies of *Acropora* and the boulders of *Porites*, while in the Atlantic the largest are *Acropora* again—the elk-horn coral—and the massive *Montastrea*. However, the many corals which bud intratentacularly show just as wide a range of shape and pattern as is found in their more numerous counterparts.

A quite different form of budding is pursued by a common but exceptional group of corals called *mushroom corals*. These are not attached to the rock but rest loosely on it. They are also found on rubble and even on sand. Most are round disks with ridges radiating outwards from a small raised dome in the centre. Others are more humped, like inverted bowls, while several species are oval rather than round. Most belong to the closely related genera *Fungia* and *Cycloseris*, although there are others as well. When very young, an attached conical polyp grows upwards, but then the stalk breaks off. The top part forms the adult disk which rolls away and it can even move about a little or right itself if turned over. The stalk which remains on the rock may either die or grow new disks. Clumps of small unattached disks may often be seen on the sea bed, in which case a search will usually find the parental stalk nearby, perhaps with a young disk still attached.

By any of these forms of budding a polyp multiplies itself. In some species, it continues until the most impressive sizes are reached. Some species of

(*Above*) The orange *Tubastraea* unfurls its tentacles at night. This one demonstrates extratentacular budding, in which new polyps simply grow from the stalk of the parent one. Here, two new daughter polyps are sprouting from the base of the central one and, although still small, they are already equipped with a full complement of food-catching tentacles.

(*Right*) *Montastrea* polyps bud in an extratentacular way so that only round cups are ever seen. This group follows *Acropora* and *Porites* in being one of the few to occur in both main coral regions. It is a very important reef builder in the Atlantic; this example is an Indo-Pacific species.

Porites can grow to form boulders over 10 metres across and containing over 100 cubic metres of rock, all originating from one polyp a millimetre across with an ability to bud. In the Caribbean, the giant elk-horn reaches even greater dimensions and such colonies may support over a million polyps and be several hundred years old, making corals the longest-lived animals on earth. Most species reach less impressive sizes, but in their large numbers they add equally to the limestone produced on the reef.

An important way in which some corals multiply and disperse happens as a result of being broken by the waves. This happens especially with branching corals. It was first thought that being broken and having branches scattered far and wide could only be harmful to the coral. But it is now clear that, for several species, the fragments which are broken and transported off can re-attach themselves to the substrate and grow into a new colony. In this way, it is quite possible for parts of one colony to end up distributed over a very wide area of reef where they eventually form many new colonies. For some, this is a major method by which they replicate themselves. The chances of survival of any particular fragment may not be too high—small rubble cays built up entirely of such fragments attest to this—but each parent may fragment repeatedly in storms so that there is a good chance that some will survive.

The polyps of many species never grow upwards. They carry on budding like all others and so their colonies only grow out sideways to form thin encrusting sheets or thin leaves, like this *Mycedium* from the Indo-Pacific.

The mushroom corals, *Fungia*, are disks which are not attached to the substrate. These are skeletons of single polyps; some are known to move around short distances and most can right themselves if turned over.

Several species can continue to grow if broken or dislodged onto sand. This species of *Acropora* relies heavily on being broken and moved by waves for its dispersal. Fragments from only one initial colony can be spread far and wide to cover many square metres where they thrive on sandy or rubble substrates.

Mixing Genes

One thing is common to both the budding and fragmentation forms of reproduction. In both cases, the genetic composition of the budded polyps and the fragmented pieces is identical to that of the parent. In a colony of coral with dozens or thousands of polyps, all are exact copies of the first polyp which settled on the substrate. Likewise, on an area of shallow reef where there is a forest of stag's-horn corals, all may have originated from one colony by fragmentation. Now, from the pattern of nature, it seems to be clearly essential that species should mix

their genes, at least occasionally. All living organisms do so and it is the essence of evolution and of how these species arose in the first place. A mixing of genes does not happen with these two methods, so a third method, and in some ways the most important method, is sexual reproduction.

An egg and sperm, each containing half the genes of a male and of a female polyp, fuse, in a similar manner to that of most other forms of life. The end result of this is a larva called a *planula*. Each colony produces hundreds of them. For most species, the planula stage is the only part of their lives when they are not attached to the rock. The planulae form a part of the plankton for many days, sometimes as long as a couple of months. During this time they drift along the reef, maybe even to another reef, and become thoroughly dispersed. Most are eaten by plankton-eating animals, but the survivors can then choose a spot to settle.

Fig. 5. This is a typical section through an atoll or a patch reef of a kind which rises from a continental shelf. To seaward (*right*) the reef plunges to the ocean floor, either continuously or in escarpments. At its top is a broad reef flat which often, but by no means always, has one or several islands on it. Behind the island (*left*) is the lagoon reef flat, followed by a slope leading down to the lagoon floor. This area is fairly sheltered. Knolls covered with corals rise off the sandy floor of the lagoon. The seaward (*right*) side also depicts a fringing reef, except in this case land would arise where just a small island is shown here and there would be no 'lagoonal' side.

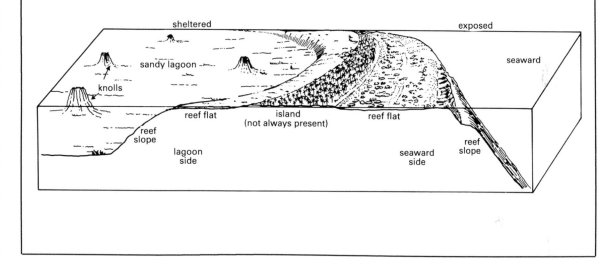

They can select their spot to some extent. They have mechanisms for sensing gravity and the direction of the light and even the nature of the substrate. They remain high up in the water column at first, then, when the time comes to settle, they head downwards. Some select bare rock, while others prefer rock which has a covering of algae. Each chooses an environment which will give it the best chance of survival in its early adult days. When it has settled, it changes into a polyp, begins to secrete a limestone case and commences to bud just like its parents. But the important thing here is that it *does* have parents—two of them—and its genetic make-up is a mixture of the genes of both.

Profile of a Reef

The net result of this budding and multiplication is the production of a lot of limestone which is used in the making of a coral reef. A reef has a typical profile or cross-section. The profile is very similar the World over. Caribbean reefs show it and so do Indo-Pacific reefs, despite the fact that the corals building them are entirely different species. Coral reefs in the central Pacific show it and so do those of the Great Barrier Reef, despite the fact that only fifty species build some of the Pacific reefs compared to over four hundred species in the richer area.

There are several things inherent in the coral reef which produce this shape. There are some other shapes, but most are only variations on this theme as a result of water conditions or the substrate. Features common to almost all are that they grow outwards, but not upwards beyond the water level, which results in a flat-topped expanse bordered by a fairly steep slope. Also, almost all contain extensive patches of sand within or behind their flat-topped regions.

Every reef can be divided up into several distinct zones. This can be done on the basis of its slope and depth or on the distribution of the different species which are attached to the bottom. In fact, the two are closely related to each other. Each part of the reef is affected by quite different amounts of such things as wave action and storm surge, or by strong heat or too little light. The life on the reef has adjusted to resist or to make best use of each of these influences and hence appears to be zoned in relation to them.

On most reefs there is a reef flat, which extends horizontally for some distance. If the reef is a fringe of coral around a volcanic island it may be only a few metres across, though on most atolls and patch reefs it can reach a width of several hundred metres. Very often corals are sparse here, as it is usually very shallow and may even dry at low tides. It may itself be divided into several inner and outer parts. Towards the outer edge of the reef flat, there may be a row of boulders thrown up by the sea. This may be followed by a ridge of slightly higher elevation than the reef flat, covered with encrusting species of red algae. Cutting through this, at the extreme outer edge of the horizontal reef, may be a series of spurs and grooves, which act as a surge system. This is the zone that takes the brunt of the waves. Following this, the reef slopes downwards, either steeply or gently, in steps or escarpments, to the lowest limit of coral growth. Sheltered reefs may also have a reef flat, but will lack the ridge and water-cut spurs or grooves at the junction of the horizontal and descending parts.

On the lagoon side of the atoll, or behind a patch reef, the slope will usually not descend as far as on the seaward side. Instead, it flattens out at moderate depths, where light is still abundant, onto a sandy or silted plain. From here rise countless mounds of rock known as *knolls* and *bommies*. They may be well-covered with corals or have good growth only on their tops, but they are often rich in many other forms of life, which contrasts strongly with the expanses of sand around them.

With small differences, the reef flat coupled with a descending reef slope is the fundamental profile of a reef. This pattern, or modification of it, can be seen on nearly all reefs. For instance, a section through the rim of an atoll shows two of these profiles back to back and this is repeated again, in mirror image, on the opposite rim of the atoll. A patch reef rising from a much shallower shelf can show it too on its exposed sides, although it may not even have an opposite rim. In miniature, this is also the shape of the coral knolls and bommies contained inside the greater structures, and most fringing reefs show the slope in its simplest form as a single stretch of flat followed by a descending slope.

The reef slopes may be steep or gentle, but are the areas of a reef which support the most coral growth. These are the parts which are growing outwards bit by bit. Their growth at the top is limited by the sea level, while growth at their lower end is gradually slowed by the falling light levels of deeper water. Growth in the shallower third of the slope is most rapid and so there is a tendency for reef slopes to grow outwards at the top. Many slopes do become vertical in parts because of this, but the dislodgement of corals, sand and chunks of reef means that much material formed in the rapidly-growing areas ends up on the deeper part. This has the effect of reducing the steepness, so on most reefs a steep but not a vertical slope is the usual configuration. The growing process is in a continual state of flux and, while it may appear to be slow in our concept of time, it is active and changing in the time-scale of the reef.

The corals are living rocks. A thin veneer of replicating, feeding, metabolising and growing tissue covers an ever-growing limestone base. The base is constantly being eroded by other life forms and by the weather, but it is this growth that provides much of the essential building materials which enables the reef to survive and grow.

Such massive structures as reefs, however, are not simply made; the corals are only one part of the story. Other groups of organisms, we shall next see, are also vital in the process of reef-building. It may be a surprise to learn later on that, over the longer term, the sand and rubble which comes from broken-down colonies of coral are just as important as the solid corals themselves in the growth and the life of the reef. One way or another, the tiny primitive polyps are a principal cause of the construction of the largest structures built by living things.

3. KINGDOM OF PLANTS

HERE HAS BEEN debate amongst scientists and students of the coral reef about its very name. The term 'coral reef', some argue, implies that the reef is built mainly by the coral animal, but botanists especially have objected that this overlooks the equally important contribution that is made by plants. It is true, of course, that corals produce a vast amount of limestone rock and it is equally true that several complicated physical and chemical processes, which we shall come to later, help to build it into a reef, but despite this the botanist can confidently state that, without the plants of the reef, there would be no reef at all.

To those who have only looked casually at a reef this may seem curious. In the coral gardens, plants, that component of life which is most conspicuous of all on land and in many other areas of the sea, are conspicuous mainly by their absence. There are no huge, fleshy brown algae, such as those which dominate the cooler waters, and only tufts here and there are visible on the reef. There are several filamentous forms and sometimes large patches of a green type called *Halimeda*, little chains of hard disks which hang from the rock. There are also small, fleshy red lumps which are clearly recognised as seaweed, and patches of red covering the rock which are not as clearly recognised but which are seaweed too. What appears to be lacking, however, is the abundant algae which we know must be there because plants are the basis of coral reef life just as they are the basis of all other living ecosystems. The answer is that the

plant mass is there, but that most of it is not immediately visible. One large part of the total plant mass is, in fact, inside the tissues of the most abundant groups of animals—the corals, soft corals and their relatives. Another part of it is in a rather unfamiliar form and one which had biologists rather confused until they managed to focus their microscopes on it. These are the calcareous red algae, fairly smooth lumps of pink stone which together can build up into massive, stony ramparts in some places. These lay down rock, just as the corals do, in some of the most wave-beaten areas of all. So, for several good reasons, the view that the most important part of a coral reef is its algae can easily be justified.

The plants of a reef are important to it in two main ways. They are the energy producers, fixing the sun's energy into a chemical form which is the basis of life the world over, and then, as we might have guessed on a coral reef built of limestone, they are important also in the limestone-depositing process.

Power Cells of the Reef

By far the most important single species of algae is a single-celled form which lies within the tissues of a wide range of animals. It is a species of dinoflagellate called *Gymnodinium microadriaticum* which exists in a condition called the *vegetative stage*. No matter what the species of coral is, or whether it is a soft coral or a sea fan, these dinoflagellates are the same through-

In any view of a coral reef, large plants are never a common sight. But the dominant organisms are the coelenterate animals—corals, soft corals and others—which farm their own plant cells within their tissues. When you look at a garden of corals you are also looking at a garden of billions of captive plant cells.

out the tropical seas. They are present in their billions and, because of their symbiotic relationship with animals, they are termed *zooxanthellae*.

They lie within the inner layer of the coral polyp's tissue and both the polyp and the algal cells obtain benefit from this remarkable relationship. Its full nature is currently a very active field of research.

Of all the species of coral in the world, about half have this symbiotic relationship with the dinoflagellate. This half, however, is the half we see on the reef; they cover the reef and build it while the corals which lack this algae mostly live in deeper water. The biology of the two groups diverges considerably as a result of the presence or absence of the zooxanthellae. The group which possesses them must live in well-lit water so that the algae can photosynthesise. This limits the corals to depths of less than 40 metres or so in most cases, although some may reach 100 metres deep. Those lacking the plant cells have no such limitation and can live in complete darkness.

Those which have the symbiotic algae, however, have developed important characteristics. They receive a tremendous nutritional benefit from the presence of their captive algal cells, part of this being that the coral containing them can grow a much bigger skeleton much more rapidly. The nutritional benefit is important not only to the coral but to the life of the reef in general, while the increased growth is important to the construction of the reef.

So great is the density of the zooxanthellae in the coral polyps that they have been estimated, in some cases, to contribute as much mass to the total living tissue of a coral as the polyps' tissue does. Therefore, when you look at a reef richly covered in corals and soft corals, a very large proportion of the living matter which you see contains a very high proportion of plant material. You are looking, in one sense, at a field of captive, single-celled algae.

Here then, is one of the main plant bases of the reef life. The algal cells are a brownish colour and this is evident almost everywhere, showing through transparent tissues and only masked when the polyp of a coral or soft coral has a strongly-coloured pigment of its own. All animal life is founded on plant life. By far the greatest quantity of animal life on the reef exists in the form of attached coelenterates: corals, soft corals, sea fans and related kinds of animals. The plant life on which they are founded is contained within their own bodies.

The ways in which each side of this partnership benefits from the presence of the other is not completely resolved, although some aspects seem clear enough. The alga almost certainly benefits from the presence of a suitable and constant environment. It takes up the metabolic wastes of the polyp, using them in its own metabolism. The carbon dioxide from the coral's respiration, for example, is required by the alga for its own photosynthesis. A waste product of that photosynthesis is oxygen and this is required by the polyp animal. Another product of the algal photosynthesis is carbohydrate and this too is used by the coral polyp. This nutritive, reciprocal relationship may exist for many other substances as well, so that there is a tight recycling of biochemicals between the animals and plants, with a very high efficiency for both partners and a minimum of waste. At no time, however, does the coral animal actually devour the algal cells themselves; it only uses their surplus products. Should the algae multiply too fast, however, then the coral polyp has the capability of getting rid of them, or a proportion of them, by expelling them from its mouth in a stream of mucus. There is evidence, in fact, that the polyp can regulate quite closely the density of algal cells in its tissue. Some can keep numbers down so that the algae form a layer just a couple of cells thick, which seems to be a level of optimum value to the coral.

In many leafy corals, the polyps are small and widely separated, connected with each other only by an extensive thin layer of tissue. This tissue also contains zooxanthellae. In all the species which contain them, the photosynthesis which takes place can supply a large proportion and perhaps most of the coral's needs. It is clear therefore that this association provides great benefit to the coral. Yet the corals still catch zooplankton to varying degrees, possibly because they need other substances which the algae cannot give them. Probably each coral species differs a little in what it needs and takes from each source. Some may take a lot of zooplankton and require little from the algae while others use mainly the algal products and take only a little plankton. It seems that the hundreds of coral species in some way share out the resources which exist, thus benefiting all sides. Furthermore, it seems that soft corals act in a similar way, dividing the total energy supply amongst themselves and the stony corals.

The benefit given by the algae does not stop at supplying food. In complex biochemical ways, which again are not well understood, the zooxanthellae enable or induce the coral polyps to deposit much greater quantities of skeleton than do corals which do not have this symbiotic association. Whether this benefits the algae is not known—it may be an

Part of the tentacle of a coral polyp, greatly magnified, showing the zooxanthellae contained inside. Each sphere is one algal cell and some dumb-bell-shaped ones are in the process of division. The diameter of each algal cell is about 0.01 millimetres. These tiny, symbiotic cells are the largest component of plant life on the reef.

This close-up is of the leafy coral, *Turbinaria*. The expanded polyps capture particles of food but occupy only a quarter of the surface. The remaining three-quarters is covered by a film of coral tissue filled with brown algal cells. This part photosynthesises very efficiently and, in terms of energy, supplies more than even the polyps. Interestingly, many corals which live in deeper and dimmer water have the greatest proportion of photosynthesising surface with a relatively tiny proportion covered by plankton-catching polyps; this emphasises the importance of light.

incidental, even accidental, result of their presence—but what is known is that this greatly increased amount of deposition creates a large part of the limestone of which the reef is made. It is true to say that the reason for this production of limestone is as much the responsibility of the zooxanthellae as it is of the polyp. The corals which contain algae are known as reef-building, or *hermatypic*, corals. Their deeper cousins, which lack algae, are not generally included in the reef-building category and are called *ahermatypic*. Some ahermatypic species are often found on the coral reef, especially on its deeper parts where a few species are common. But generally, without algae, they cannot contribute in the same way to the building process.

The main plant component of the coral reef in the region where most coral lives, therefore, is not seen in a casual look. It may be microscopic in its form, but its total quantity is immense. There is plant tissue over the entire coral garden, where there is an average of $1\frac{1}{2}$ million of these tiny cells for every square centimetre of coral surface and perhaps a hundred billion every square metre of the convoluted surface of the reef. Every new reef-building coral which grows contains this alga from the start, because cells of it are carried over from the parent to the larva. The reef therefore does have a lot of plant mass on which its animals are biologically supported.

Colours for Growth

Most of the plant life consists of this single species, but the remaining portion is made up of many

These are fast-growing tips of a species of the coral *Acropora*. The new tips are still pale because they lack the brown algal cells. About 1 centimetre down (the tips shown are about 3 centimetres long), the tissue looks brown and filled with algal cells. A few weeks later, new algal cells will have moved up to occupy the new coral tissue.

(*Left*) The table-shaped coral colony of *Acropora* on which the diver is resting his hand has a pale rim while the rest of the table and all the others are brownish green. This table rim is growing very rapidly outwards and is pale because the brown-coloured algal cells have not yet moved out to occupy the new coral tissue.

(*Right*) This tuft of green algae forms its own calcareous stalk and grows out of sand. This makes it one of the relatively few large plants which are found on sand rather than on rock. Called *Pennicillus*, it grows on both Indo-Pacific reefs and, like this example, in the Caribbean.

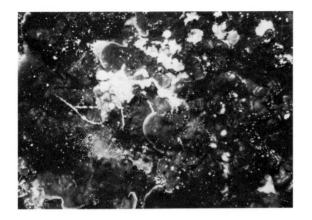

Some of the commonest red algae are the thin, delicate plates found encrusting much of the rock in moderate and deep areas of the reef. These thrive in places where the light is too dim for many other life forms, partly because they have a slow metabolic rate and do not require much energy.

Where a patch of fleshy algae exists there is often a reason why it has not been cropped. This damsel fish, *Abudefduf*, is one common reason. Inside an invisible boundary to its territory, it will bite and buffet anything which intrudes, including a diver's hand. Grazing fish flee and the algae grows.

hundreds of other types. We can see several different colours of seaweed on the reef and this reflects their major groupings.

Seaweeds, or algae, are a fairly primitive sort of plant by nature and they come in several types. World-wide, the biggest are coloured brown and, while these dominate in colder seas, they are relatively scarce and small in the tropics. The greens are another group. They are fairly common on reefs and they include a wide range of shapes, from low bushes to thin filaments. The largest group on the reefs are red algae. These appear on the coral reef in a wide variety of shapes and forms. Some are jelly-like and delicate while others lay down limestone in a similar manner to the corals.

The many species of these groups, the greens, reds and browns, make up almost all the algae which we see on the reef. There are others too—we have seen that a group of tiny blue-greens is important for fixing nitrogen—and there are other rather inconspicuous forms as well. Some of the microscopic forms which occur in the plankton fall into still more groups. All of these are of considerable importance, but in terms of quantity they are not a major part of the plant life of the reef.

The colours are the result of different pigments within the cells of the plants. The pigments have a

major role to play in trapping the light and in the photosynthesis which then occurs in the plant. Some pigments allow the plant to utilise low light levels or to make use of certain wavelengths (or colours) of light. The availability of both wavelength and intensity of light is changed by the amount of water through which the light has to pass, so the various pigments can permit the plants which possess them to expand their range. As a result, some plants can live on the reef in sometimes considerable abundance below a depth of 60 or even 100 metres. Down there, the red algae in particular manage to survive very well.

Still, although we can see a lot of different sorts of seaweed if we look carefully, there do not seem to be very many of them in terms of quantity and the reef clearly does lack the massive standing crops which we see in colder waters. Yet there are a lot of herbivorous animals on the bottom and a lot of grazing fish above them which depend on seaweed, so how do they survive? The answer is that the seaweed grows very rapidly but is eaten just as rapidly by the herbivores. As soon as some appears it is immediately eaten, so the turnover is very fast.

As a result, there is never a vast build-up of seaweed. Measurements have shown that, in the well-lit areas of the coral reef, as much as 1 or 5 kilograms of

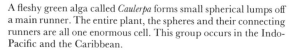

A fleshy green alga called *Caulerpa* forms small spherical lumps off a main runner. The entire plant, the spheres and their connecting runners are all one enormous cell. This group occurs in the Indo-Pacific and the Caribbean.

(*Above right*) The Caribbean sea slug, *Tridachia crispata*, feeds on seaweed. Not only does it obtain food but it uses the plant's energy-fixing chloroplasts for its own ends. These structures are not digested but are absorbed whole and relocated onto the slug's back where they continue to photosynthesise and produce food substances for the animal.

(*Below*) Two stone-producing plants. The green alga (*left*) is *Halimeda* and the pink stone (*right*) is a typical growth of the stony red alga of the *Porolithon* and *Lithothamnion* group. Only a thin layer of the surface is plant tissue and this continually deposits limestone beneath itself in a way which is probably essentially similar to corals. Single plants may grow into very large lumps.

seaweed can grow in a year on every square metre. At any one moment, however, it is unlikely that more than a few grams exists, because, when it does, the herbivorous parrot fish or surgeon fish or the grazing sea urchins quickly crop it down to the bare rock again. In the World generally, most fish are carnivo-

rous, but the coral reef has a greater proportion of herbivores than most areas. This means that the edible forms of fleshy seaweed never build up to high standing stocks, but they still provide a large part of the plant food of the reef.

We can see how fast this nutritious algae grows simply by making sure the grazers are kept away from it. Experiments have been done using small cages placed over a patch of reef to keep everything out. It is not long before tufts of green filaments and fleshy red algae grow to cover the entire patch. There are other ways in which grazers are prevented access to the algae, this time by natural means. Next time you see a patch covered with algae, look for a damsel fish, a beau-gregory or another fish with a strong sense of territory nearby. It is quite likely that one will be clearly in evidence, defending its patch of territory from every intruder, including you. The little damsel fish may only be a few centimetres long, but it has the determination of a bulldog at a postman's ankle as it buffets and bites any intruder, regardless of size. If you put your hand in its territory, be prepared for it to have a go at you too. By its actions, it repels herbivorous animals and, as a result, the algae grows ungrazed within the strongly defended domains of the little fish.

In many areas, the green algae, *Halimeda*, may be very common. These are calcareous algae, meaning they too deposit limestone in their tissues. As a result, they are sand-producers and, in that context, they reappear later in Chapter 8. Their abundance is largely due to the fact that they do produce limestone. This makes their substance mostly rock and rather unacceptable as food to most grazers. There is one brown alga, the fan-shaped *Padina*, which also deposits limestone. Most calcareous algae, however, are red, and it is plants of this group which produce the most remarkable stony structures.

Pink Stones

A friend of mine, who has wide-ranging knowledge of the natural sciences but who is unashamedly a botanist, once said that he regarded colonies of coral animals as being honorary plants. He was referring to their light-requiring behaviour and to their dependence on symbiotic plant cells and it was said only partly in jest. Those plant cells do control to a large degree where the coral can grow. They do also greatly increase the deposition of rock by the coral polyps. But, in the deposition of limestone, the calcareous red algae are also of the greatest importance and they deposit it directly. So it was that another friend of mine, this time a geologist, claimed them all as honorary rocks.

This demonstrates the total interdependence of animals and plants and their own self-created substrate. None make what we know as a coral reef on their own, but the calcareous red algae hold a place of great importance.

They are particularly conspicuous on reefs which are very exposed to waves, at the point where the reef flat dips down to continue as a submerging reef slope. Here there is a pink ridge, made and covered by living calcareous red algae. These algae do not at all match our ideas of how a seaweed should look. They are mostly limestone, deposited by the cells of the plant tissue. In terms of weight, these rounded stones are 95% rock and only 5% living organic tissue. The living part is near to, and on, the surface of its rock where its pigments give it all a pink colour. The countless growths fuse into one another, with frequent, richer red nodules showing where very healthy growth occurs. These algae are mainly of the genus *Porolithon* in the Indo-Pacific, joined by *Litho-thamnion* in the Caribbean. They thrive in the region where the waves smash onto the reef with greatest force, and it seems that they need this violence for best growth. The result of their growth is a broad ridge, called the *algal ridge*, which can grow several kilometres in length as it runs parallel to the edge of the reef. It can reach to about half a metre above the low-tide level but is always covered with water, even on lowest tides, as it is continually flooded by the surge of the ocean swell or by the foam of the breakers. It is very rare to find corals here and only these cement-strong plants make and protect the reef in its most turbulent places.

At the seaward edge of the ridge are spurs, made of the same red algae, projecting many metres out to sea. On a typical reef, these may be a couple of metres broad, each separated from adjacent ones by a gap of about the same distance. This area is known as the *spurs and grooves*. The algae-constructed spurs may project 75 metres out to sea, tapering downwards into deeper water until a point is reached a few metres deep where the turbulence is too little to support these algae. Backwash from every wave pours back through the grooves, keeping their floors swept clear of any life and making settlement of new life impossible. (The same term 'spurs and grooves', may be used for the edges of other reefs where very similar structures exist which are not caused by algal growth. The configuration is the same but the grooves are simply cut into the bedrock of the reef. The backwash of the waves, given scouring power by suspended sand, cuts a very similar pattern.)

How this pattern results is not really known, but one of its consequences is far-reaching. If you stand on the ridge at low tide and look out along a groove, it is possible to see one of the ways in which the tremendous energy of the waves is absorbed and made less harmful. The length and spacing of the algal spurs is such that, under typical conditions, the wall of backwash flooding down a groove back to the sea from one wave meets the oncoming breaker of the next wave. The two collide somewhere in the middle in a froth of foam and turbulence, partly cancelling each other out. Were it not for this, the destructive force would be considerably greater and the energy from millions of kilowatts that would hit each kilometre of the reef would probably be too great even for these remarkable, stony algae.

These growths are the reason why many reefs can

In stormy positions, such as at the seaward edge of the reef flat, calcareous red algae thrive. Countless stony plants of *Porolithon* in the Indo-Pacific, joined by *Lithothamnion* in the Caribbean, grow to make huge ridges up to 1 metre high, 30 metres wide and running the length of the reef. Projecting seaward are spurs made by the same algae. In this example, the ridge is exposed at low tide and spurs run outwards, continuing beneath the breaking waves for a total of 50 metres.

Sea grasses are higher than algae in an evolutionary sense, but are rare sights at any depth on a coral reef. In shallow waters and on or behind reef flats, however, they can occur in very large, thick beds. This one is *Thalassodendron* on a reef flat.

exist at all in their present state. Of course, they are eroded all the time by the abrasion which they face and continually have chunks knocked off by storm waves, but the algal ridge and spurs continue to keep themselves in good repair.

At a few metres deep these algae largely disappear and there is a gap where red algae are far fewer and where the greens especially exceed them in terms of growth. As still greater depths are reached, however, the reds come back again in force. Different species this time; the new inhabitants are thin, encrusting sheets of red tissue of various sizes. It is sometimes difficult to distinguish them from some of the thin red sponges which live alongside them, but the plants are often duller in colour and have a different texture. On the deepest parts of the reef, they grow well and can get by with very little light. They are efficient at photosynthesis, but they do not require much energy as they grow very slowly and it is this that seems to be the key to their success in dark areas. They add to the food base of the reef just as all plants do, but where they also make their mark is in their ability to grow over pockets of trapped sediment which later results in a solidifying of the sediment into hard rock. This too helps the reef to grow and maintain itself in the face of continuous erosion, this time mainly from boring animals. But there comes a point when it becomes too dark even for these slow-growers and the growth of plants eventually ceases. Below this depth there is no coral reef community as we know it and the animal life is supported now either directly or indirectly by food material which falls down to this region from the lighted areas above. Life below the lighted zone is always much more sparse.

Green Meadows

The plants which you see underwater when diving on a reef are mostly algae. They are primitive plants which are mainly confined to marine or freshwater environments because they do not have mechanisms to prevent themselves from drying out. Some algae are found on land, but only in damp areas. Most land plants are higher plants, much more recently evolved in terms of life's long span. They can not only resist drying out but have also developed different and more complicated structures for obtaining their minerals and for reproduction. They include the flowering plants; from, minute, leafy herbs, through grasses, to trees. Some which resemble grasses can now be found in the sea.

Sea grasses are important plants on some coral reefs. In sheltered water in particular, they can exist in patches, and even huge meadows, covering large areas. Another name for one type of sea grass is turtle grass, as it supplies turtles with a part of their diet. Sea grasses mainly inhabit fairly shallow water and the chief areas in which they are found are not on reefs at all but on sandy and muddy flats and bays. Where the conditions and substrate are right for

them, however, they will also colonise parts of coral reefs. This usually means the tops of reefs on the extensive reef flats or perhaps in the shallows between the land and a fringing reef just offshore.

These are plants which have returned to living in the sea after their ancestors developed adaptations which allowed them to move out of it and onto land. They still retain a wide range of structures not seen in other marine plants. These include flowers which bloom under water, although they are now small and rather inconspicuous structures. Another terrestrial adaptation which they have are roots.

Roots were needed for living on land. Algae do not have them as they can absorb the water and minerals they need for life, through their filaments and fronds, directly from the sea water which bathes them. The higher land plants do not have the advantage of such a benign medium and so obtain their needs through structures which at the same time anchor the plants in the soil. This is the key to the different sorts of environments in which sea grasses are found; they need some kind of soil to grow in and cannot live on the solid surfaces which are home to algae. The sandy, muddy places which are suitable for them are often shallow and are almost always flat expanses where the waves are not too strong. In such places, sea grasses thrive, stabilising the muddy areas and permitting the existence of a community of animals which depend on them for food and shelter. These areas can be very significant to a reef by providing plant material and nursery grounds.

However, throughout the seas as a whole, only a minority of coral reefs have extensive areas of sea grass. On most, the algae are still the principal foundation of the animal life, just as they were on ancient reefs before the sea grasses ever appeared amongst the kingdom of plants. From the single floating cells in the plankton and the single captive cells in the corals to the large areas of pink-coloured stone, the marine algae are the main group of plants on the coral reef.

So it is not surprising that, on very wave-battered reefs in particular, it has been suggested that the term 'algal reef' is as accurate as 'coral reef' in describing these teeming structures of the sunlit, tropical seas.

4. PLATFORMS IN THE SHALLOWS

AT HIGH TIDE you can take a small boat across the top of almost any coral reef in the world. For a few hours each day, the clearance should be sufficient to prevent you from hitting the propeller of your boat on the corals which live on the top of the reef but, as the tide begins to drop, so does the gap above the sharp and solid corals until, at low spring tide, the reef is high and dry. The reef flats of atolls, the tops of any patch reef on a continental shelf and the tops of every fringing reef find their position at about the average low-tide mark.

It is not difficult to see why all living reefs should have this uppermost boundary. Quite simply, the organisms and processes which make them are marine and cannot grow or do not work outside the water. Parts of many reefs do protrude, but as we have seen, these are either remnants of ancient rock still not eroded back to water level or else piles of sand and debris heaped up by the waves. Either way, they are not currently living in the sense we mean here.

This flat expanse lying at low-water level is the largest part of many reefs. On a fringing reef, it may extend some distance out from the shore before a point is reached where the reef slope plummets downwards. In particular, patch reefs which rise from shallow water and atolls which rise from deep water have extensive horizontal expanses of reef flats. (They may enclose still greater areas of sandy lagoon, but the reef flat is the largest expanse of hard reef.) It is the area of the coral world which is the

most accessible to the casual viewer, because at low tide it is easy to walk out onto it from the shore or island from which it extends. In days not so long ago, when very few people had seen or studied the deeper, richer slopes beyond the reef flat, almost all coral reef research was limited to this part. Because of this, for many, the reef flat was simply called the reef and, should you read some older books on reefs, be careful to notice when the author is only referring to what we

A part of a reef flat at high tide. About a metre of clear water covers the corals, rubble and sand patches with their numerous small invertebrates. Many flats, like this one, are stepped and irregular, due to eroding streams of water as the tide ebbs and flows twice each day. The extreme high-tide level is marked on the islands by the lower limit of the vegetation.

now regard as the reef flat—just one component, and a rather exceptional one, of a much more complex structure. As seen from above, it may be the largest area in many cases, and seamen who speak of reefs are still entirely justified in being concerned only about these parts which lie within the draft of their ships. However, from the viewpoint of the life of the reef, it is the poorest part, with fewest species, and many reef flats support very little life at all.

This is the area where the living, growing coral reef is cut off and shaped by the interface of sea and air and, as such, it is of great importance geologically. It is an interesting area, an extreme outpost of many deeper marine species and a home for several more which have specialised in living in this harsh environment. To us, even in these days of aqualungs, it is still the part of the reef with easiest access and where we can spend the most time and it tells us a lot about the reef as a whole and its life.

Visible and Invisible Light

It is the visible light from the sun which drives the life of a coral reef, just as it drives all other living systems, by providing the energy which is used in photosynthesis. At sea level in the tropics, this light is usually intense. A thickness of water cuts this down, but it is a characteristic of reef flats that there is very little water lying on top of them—a metre or two at high tide and just a couple of centimetres or even none at all at low tide. By itself, the intense visible light of the sun does not harm the life of the reef flat.

Another part of the same seaward-facing reef flat, but at extreme low tide. Much of it is dry and baked in the noon sun and, where there is water, it is only a few centimetres deep and is cut off from the ocean. Its temperature rapidly becomes unpleasantly hot for us and lethal to most reef-dwelling species. Several small invertebrates do live here, but the flats of this Indian Ocean atoll are relatively barren.

The level of light here is far more than is necessary for maximum photosynthesis but complex biochemical mechanisms take place in the plants to prevent themselves from burning out because of this surfeit of a good thing and many plants can thrive under these conditions.

More than visible light pours from the sun. Visible light is just a tiny fraction of the spectrum of energy, ranging from X-rays to radio-waves, which beat down on the reef flat. Most parts of it are harmless and unnoticed by the life there. There are kinds of radiation, however, which are very harmful in excess and it is the sun's wavelengths which lie on either side of the visible part which are the most harmful of all.

Ultra-violet light is that part of the spectrum sometimes called *black light*. We cannot see it (although some insects can) but we can see its effects when it shines onto many materials and chemicals making them glow with visible light. An indication of how harmful this type of radiation can be is that it includes cancer-causing wavelengths and is used for sterilising purposes in laboratories where micro-organisms are used. Ultra-violet radiation has a marked effect on the species of the reef flat. Many marine animals are killed by it and it appears that those which can survive in the exposed shallow positions are those which have developed some resistance to its lethal effects in ways which are still unknown. A favoured mode of life amongst the animals which do live there, such as the numerous brittle stars, is to live in cracks and crevices. This may well be to hide from this type of radiation. Attached species, however, cannot move into crevices during the daytime and these must resist this radiation to survive.

Ultra-violet wavelengths are shorter than those of visible light. Wavelengths longer than visible light begin with infra-red and this means heat. Heat and its associated effects, such as drying, are the most important hostile condition which reef-flat life has to cope with.

It is around low tide when the strong heating action of the tropical sun has most effect. Before the water level falls, there is a good exchange of sea water across the reef flat. The action of waves breaking at its edge causes cooler water from the open sea to pump across it, washing off the water which is warmed by the sun and replacing it with new oceanic water. As the tide falls, less water covers the organisms on the reef flat and less water is pumped over them so the temperature rises. Ponding may occur in many places until, at the lowest tides, many areas are cut off from the water flow completely and have only a few centimetres to cover them. Temperatures here shoot upwards into the 30s and even 40s centigrade.

When marine life is warmed up, it needs more oxygen to remain alive. It is a physical fact, however, that warm water can contain less dissolved oxygen than cool water, so the combined effects of a greater oxygen demand and a reduced availability of oxygen happen together. In these circumstances, the water is literally suffocating. In addition, evaporation results in the water becoming dangerously salty. This too increases the stress to life and the combined effects of all these factors make the environment of the reef flat a very hostile place for life. The parts of the reef

A lagoonward-facing reef flat at the lowest tide of the year is entirely dry and elevated several centimetres above sea level. From island beach to the edge of the reef flat is 100 metres and, at the rather abrupt edge of the flat, the reef slopes sharply downwards.

flat that end up just above the water fare even less well. This can happen to much of the reef flat on a low spring tide and to slightly elevated parts of it more often still. Such parts become thoroughly dehydrated and, when unpredictable climatic events result in a particularly low tide coinciding with an overhead sun, a reef flat whose life has slowly built up over a long period can be devastated again. It is characteristic of reef flats that their living com-

A reef flat on part of the Great Barrier Reef at very low tide. Flats in this region differ markedly from those illustrated previously by having a very high cover of corals. Relatively few species have enough resistance to tolerate the heat and dessication which these corals are currently suffering, but those which can live here clearly do very well. Such exposure may last 2–3 hours before the tide rises again.

High tide brings an oxygenated, cool, protective layer of water to this reef flat of the Great Barrier Reef with its high cover of corals. The infra-red rays of the sun are completely barred by even this 1 metre depth, although ultra-violet rays can still penetrate.

munities suffer periodic destructions whose frequencies depend on climatic and tidal cycles.

A danger to the life may come also from quite a different source. Just as increased salinity caused by evaporation is harmful, so is decreased salinity caused by dilution. Torrential rain at low tides dilutes the salt content of the water and may even completely replace the ponded areas with fresh water. By a process called *osmosis*, living tissues cannot help but absorb more water. Cells rupture under the strain and damage to the tissues results. Because heavy rain is a common feature of many areas of the tropics, this is an important problem which is faced by the life on the reef flats.

The dangerous period may last for just a few hours. As the tide rises again more benign conditions return. Cooler water flows in across the reef, bringing with it plenty of dissolved oxygen and a salt content that is just right for marine life. Exposed parts are immersed again and temperatures fall as the heated water is flushed off the reef flat and away into the open sea. You may see extensive flocs of mucus floating on the surface at this time, secreted by the corals during the stressful period and now being washed away.

The tidal situation is very important. The worst extremes do not occur every day and respite comes from the fact that tides move forward half an hour or more every day. So, for a large part of every lunar cycle, the lowest tides do not occur when the sun is strongest. Also, less extreme neap tides alternate with springs so that, for most days in each month, the water level stays high enough to keep all life fairly well-covered. Even when conditions could be severe, sometimes thick cloud cover can prevent the worst from happening. However, it is the lowest tides on hot, clear days which mainly govern what may live here, as it is during these periods when the invisible radiation from the sun pours down onto the life, unchecked by a revitalising supply of sea water.

Adjusting to Life

To live here, some species of animals and plants have developed mechanisms for resisting heat and dehydration and osmotic stress resulting from both too much and too little salt in the water. These species must also be able to cope with low oxygen levels for at least 2 or 3 hours at a time. Also, they must tolerate large and rapid fluctuations of all these stresses, something to which it is often much more difficult to adjust than a steady stress.

A great deal of variability exists on reef flats. Many areas on the Great Barrier Reef, for example, show a very high cover of corals, while others of some Indian Ocean atolls are nearly bare, showing vast expanses of uncolonised limestone slabs. But, even where there is a large quantity of life, there are far fewer species than in areas which do not suffer these environmental extremes. Several corals may do quite well, particularly boulder and encrusting forms. Where the reef flats are sufficiently distant from severe wave action, the table corals of *Acropora* may be dominant. Sheet-like sponges encrust the rock while the soft cups which dot the area are sponges called *Phyllospongia*. Brittle stars are remarkably abundant in crevices, while sea cucumbers lie on the rock or on and underneath sandy patches which are scattered over the flat expanses. Gastropod molluscs, especially

For about three-quarters of each day, the depth of water over the reef flat is sufficient for fish to swim. Sting rays, like this species of Dasyatidae, traverse the flats and sleep in its sandy patches. They are mostly seen only when disturbed.

(*Top*) A deadly inhabitant of reef flats, especially rubble-covered parts, is the well-camouflaged scorpion fish shown here and the even more poisonous stone fish. These lie motionless and, if stepped upon, will inject venom by means of spines on their back. Strong-soled shoes are essential for reef walking, day or night.

(*Above*) The six-armed starfish, *Linkia*, is a common inhabitant of reef flats, here foraging in the boulder zone of a reef flat where mounds of coral fragments are tossed by waves.

drupes, cones and cowries, are relatively common, most living concealed during the day and emerging only at night. Species which have adapted to these conditions may enjoy some advantages, however, as they may suffer less competition from others and less predation.

The types of life that we see here are of two main sorts: those which live here either exclusively, or nearly so, and those to whom the reef flat is at the extreme of their normal living range. The first group is the smallest, but there are several species of corals, molluscs and brittle stars, for example, which are mainly found here. They are well adapted to the harsh conditions with which the majority of species find it too difficult to cope, and hence they do not face such severe competition from other species as do those which live in the less extreme and even benign areas slightly deeper down. It is on the reef flat that, with their particular capabilities, they find it best to live and they may not even be able to survive in areas where the majority of species occur.

The other group found here are *outliers*, individuals of species which have a wider range of habitats but which are centred on another usually deeper area. Some members of their population appear up here, although they rarely grow as well or as large as they can do deeper down. It is probably true that, if you search for long enough on enough reef flats, there will be few coral-reef species that you could never eventually find. You will find a few and even many examples of a lot of them, but they will be outliers from their preferred areas where they live more abundantly and successfully.

It is on the reef flat that coral colonies of many species grow into shapes called *micro-atolls*. As their name implies, these are small rings of living coral of one colony which have grown into the shape of an atoll, as a result of the influence of low tides. It starts when a boulder coral, or almost any other form, grows in a normal fashion to form a small colony. When it reaches a certain size, the top is exposed at a low tide and is killed, but the sides are unaffected and continue to grow outwards. The circle grows larger and larger, but it can never grow upwards any further. The dead top commonly becomes eroded too, which emphasises its dish or atoll shape even

(*Above*) In well-sheltered areas of reef flats and on the tops of protected coral knolls, complicated patterns of growth and erosion cause deep pockets. Fast-growing corals occupy them, although occasional storms smash growths such as these and scatter the fragments.

(*Left*) These are micro-atolls on the flats of a fringing reef. The corals are colonies of hardy *Goniastrea*, whose tops are killed by frequent exposure to air and sun, but whose sides continue to grow outwards. Small colonies may form rings of living coral, but older ones, as here, become series of large, sometimes disconnected arcs.

more. Many of the species which can tolerate reef-flat conditions may be seen as micro-atolls. If a colony growing in this way manages to reach a large size of a few metres in diameter, its patterns of growth become more complex. Often the perfect circles seen in small cases break up. They become convoluted and disconnected, with arcs and secondary circles developing beside and within the earlier growths. The largest ones may reach several metres from one end to the other when seen from above, but their height is always limited to the distance between the substrate and the low tide mark and their total amount of living surface is rarely very great.

Even fossil corals in fossil reefs have been found in these configurations and this has given strong evidence of the heights of past sea levels in relation to the reef; series of such structures help to show how the sea level has changed over the last several thousand years.

Rising Turbulence

As the edge of an exposed and seaward-facing reef flat is approached, the changes in its surface and in the life upon it become more marked. On stormy reefs, a *boulder zone* is reached, where coral colonies, now dead, and even chunks of reef, have been thrown up by the sea. This area is often piled up quite high above the rest of the reef flat and is the first part to break surface as the tide falls. No corals and only very hardy crevice-dwellers live here.

Going further outwards on the exposed reef there is then another short stretch which is a little deeper than the rest of the reef flat, which has earned it the name of the *moat*. This part is assured a better exchange of water than the other parts of the reef flat because it is closer to the breaking waves themselves. It receives the water which is pumped onto the top before the other sections and more species of coral can usually be found here, with sponges and algae too. But a change is now found in the factors which mainly control which species and how much life find it possible to live. The destructive effects of drying out and high temperatures diminish since surges of water continually flood the area. Instead, however, the waves which keep this part better covered than the rest begin to have a much stronger, direct impact. For corals to be found here, they must be sturdy forms not easily broken, even when waves break directly on them, and they must equally well withstand constant surges as the water pumps and ebbs across them. Many species of corals and other animals do live here and, perhaps surprisingly, several are branched forms, such as the sturdy *Stylophora* and several *Acropora*.

The moat is not the most turbulent of all the reef-flat zones. That position is reserved for the one at the outermost edge of the reef flat, termed the *reef crest*. This area is affected and shaped by the waves which crash upon it in several complex ways. In atolls, for example, the crest is at its most prominent when the wave energy which hits it is at its most severe. This is because, in these cases, the growth of calcareous red algae flourishes, building up conspicuous pink-coloured ridges which run along the outermost edge. These can readily be seen in many areas in all three tropical oceans, but, in many places, the structures are poorly developed or even absent, even when the wave energy seems to be high enough. It depends partly on the geographical position and on other still unknown conditions which either encourage or prevent the growth of the vast algal ramparts. In calmer, more protected conditions, the algal ridges do not grow at all. In that case, there may still be a boulder zone some metres inwards from the edge, but then only a short, flat stretch before a downward slope marks the end of the reef flat. On still more sheltered reef flats there is no boulder zone either.

On lagoonward-facing reef flats of an atoll, or on some fringing reefs for example, the change from reef flat to reef slope can be less sudden as one merges slowly into the other with a very gradually-steepening slope. In such cases, the cover of corals and the diversity of all forms of life build up slowly too. If the waves in these places rarely reach destructive power, then a great profusion of more delicately branching forms may dominate the surface of the rock, until the surface rock cannot be seen at all for its canopy of corals.

From the air, the only part of most coral reefs which can clearly be seen is the reef flat, with, in many cases, islands placed upon it and bright sandy

ocean
(~500m)

spurs

spurs

village

lagoon
(25m)

patches to leeward of it in water of increasing depth. The steeper reef slopes beyond it are only hinted at by a narrow line of greens sandwiched between the bright reef flat and the blue of very deep water. In the lagoon of relatively shallow water behind the reef flat will be many roughly circular patches which mark the tops of coral knolls, variously termed *patches* or *bommies*, of many sizes. The tops of these reflect in miniature the larger flats, and their living communities suffer from the ultra-violet and infra-red of the sun in exactly the same way. Being in the sheltered lagoons, though, they rarely suffer from the stormy conditions experienced by the seaward reefs and so may be dominated by more fragile, branching corals. All these rise up towards the surface from the sea floor, mostly to the low-tide mark where the interface of sea and air halts their upward but not their outward growth.

From the air, the reef flats stand out clearly but, for all their great expanse, the hostility of the en-

Part of an atoll rim showing seaward and lagoonward reef flat connected by more reef flat between the islands. The line of white breakers at the top edge continually pumps water across the flat which runs between the islands and into the lagoon. The white surf conceals the algal ridge but spurs are visible in two places. The water flow between these islands reaches 5 knots and has caused two sand banks to tail into the lagoon. The sheltered lagoon reef flat has no line of surf. Stripes on the flats are alternating areas of coral, rubble and sand, caused by water movement.

vironment on their surface limits the number of coral species and other forms of life which can grow there. Beyond them on the reef slopes is where the greater variety of coral reef life begins. All the same, it is the shallows of the reef flat which we can spend the most time looking at. Like the rest of the reef and its living systems, it is constantly changing, too slowly for us to easily measure, as it grows outwards in some parts and is eroded back in others. It offers us a great deal which is both spectacular and of great interest.

51

5. THE INFINITE VARIETY

NOBODY can tell with any degree of accuracy how many species of animals and plants exist on the coral reefs of the world. For the oceans as a whole some rough estimates have been made, and some guesses suggest that there are about 15 000 species of marine algae and about half a million marine animals. That is, there are about thirty to forty species of animal to each species of plant. (On land also there are many more species of animal than plant, although here the numbers of both plants and animals are over ten times greater than in the sea.)

This applies to the whole oceanic world with its shallow bays, deep oceans, rocky shorelines and vast expanses of mud as well as reefs. But the location of this half-million-odd species is not uniform by any means. Shallow waters have more species than deeper waters. Rocky areas have more than sandy and muddy areas, and the tropics contain more species than colder seas. Coral reefs fall into the richest category of all. They are shallow, tropical and rocky, and may support about a quarter or so of all marine species. However, as it is still a fact that a vast number of species have yet to be found and identified, this can be little more than a guess. All we can say with any accuracy is that coral reefs are apparently the richest areas of all in the seas in terms of different forms of life.

This enormous number of different species, most of which are animals, poses quite a problem for us in our understanding of the reef. All species differ from all others to some degree, otherwise they would not

be different species. So to enable us to understand the workings of the reef life in general and its enormous number of different parts, it helps to be able to group them into just a few categories. The groups which we end up with may be rather loosely defined and ragged around the edges, but the end result is a small number of groups which we can visualise and understand instead of the tens of thousands of interacting parts which we start with.

We can do this, for example, with the way the reef life feeds. We have made categories which we term *carnivore* and *herbivore*, *suspension-feeder* or *detritus-feeder* and a few others. Many species fall into a single category while many span two or maybe even three. But even though many species do not fall conveniently into one of our categories we have achieved a simplification which allows us to understand better the feeding structure of reef life which would have been rather difficult otherwise.

The feeding structure of the reef is one of the most important aspects of the reef life to understand. Feeding is, after all, one of the basic requirements of life and, if we can see how the food web on a coral reef operates, at least in broad principle, then we are well on the way to understanding many other aspects of it as well.

There may well be thirty species of animal for every species of plant, but this tells only one part of the story. As we have seen, all animals are totally dependent on plants for their nutrition, even if they are carnivores, as their prey or their prey's prey will ultimately be a plant-eater. If we look not at the number of species but at their *biomass* (which literally means amount or mass of living substance) then the ratio of animals to plants is reversed: in fact, the total biomass of plant life produced per year on a reef is ten times greater than the amount of animal life which grows. There may be fewer species of plant but there is more plant life as a whole.

Pyramids of Life

The organic material produced by the plants of the reef is known as the *primary production*. It is the primary and direct consequence of the process whereby the energy of the sun is converted into biological structures. The plant cells and the complex proteins and carbohydrates within them, the connective tissue holding the cells together, and a lot of dissolved chemicals which seep out into the seawater, are all part of the primary productivity.

Most of the primary productivity, or plant life, is, as we have seen, locked up in the tissues of the coelenterate animals in the shape of billions of zooxanthellae. The remainder, we saw, is not particularly abundant at any one time, because although it grows quickly it is also eaten quickly so that large stocks of it never build up. These plants together form the base of all the food chains on the reef and all the food chains can be combined and viewed schematically as a pyramid.

Plants form the base of this pyramid of life. In the now classical version, herbivores form the next layer up. Carnivores, which eat the herbivores form the layer on top of that. Then there are higher, or second order, carnivores like the barracuda, moray eels and, of course, the shark. These eat the lower level carnivores and so form a layer above the rest; we may call them the *secondary carnivore* level.

In this simple pyramid, things are governed by a few simple rules. First there is the rule that it *is* a pyramid or conical shape and no other structure. Each level upwards, or each layer more distant from the plants at the base of it all, is much smaller than the one beneath it. In fact, there is an energy loss of about nine-tenths between one level and the next.

Translated, this means that an organism uses up nine-tenths of all the food it ever obtains for living purposes—for moving and breeding for example. Only one-tenth is turned into tissue which may be used as food for anything which eats it. So, in a very real sense, the amount of life at any one level puts a clear limit on the size and abundance at the next level up. Also, because there is a reduction of nine-tenths at each step, it does not take very many steps before the percentage of the initial energy which is left becomes vanishingly small and quite incapable of supporting any more levels. That is why, on a reef, there is and must be a smaller amount of herbivores than of plants, a smaller amount of carnivores than of herbivores, and still smaller amounts of higher level carnivores.

However, more accurately, this does not strictly mean the amount which *exists*, but rather the amount which is *produced*. A plant for example, may have a very fast growth rate, but if it is eaten so rapidly that it never gets a chance to build up into large growths, it will have a small presence at any one time. It still has a high production however. So it is the production which counts, not simply the bulk. When production is measured in order to gain an understanding of the life on the reef, both existing bulk and its rate of turnover must be included in the estimates. If this is done, we see that the net production by plants on reef—that is, the amount available for animals to eat—may be as much as 1 to 2 kilograms per year for every square metre of reef surface.

We have said that the coral reef has more different types of life on it for a given area than any other ecosystem in the sea and that each of our feeding categories is rather rough and ready. So it is not surprising that there is considerable mixing of the feeding levels of the pyramid; you can see many examples of this just by looking around on a dive. A carnivorous fish may eat a different species every day for weeks, sometimes taking herbivores, sometimes various levels of carnivores. The predatory cone shell, or volute, may catch other molluscs, crustaceans or worms, which are herbivores, carnivores, or detritus (debris) feeders. Anything which eats a coral takes in both the animal and its captive plant cells. And what of a coral itself which feeds on planktonic larvae of every conceivable species and also depends on algae growing within itself? It is impossible to draw clear levels in the pyramid.

To make things simpler still we can reduce life to just two major categories: the primary producers, which means the plants, and the secondary producers, which means all the rest. Two categories should be fairly easy to understand in principle.

Unfortunately, the link between the plants and animals of the reef is one of the current mysteries of how the system works. We know a lot about the plants and we know a lot about the animals, but we know very little of how the energy of the plants actually supports the dazzling array of animals. More technically, how is the secondary production supported by the primary production? Some animals eat the plants but there are really not very many of these compared to the whole animal population. Quite simply, there seem to be too few herbivores.

Amongst the fish, for example, which we know to be a very important, dominant and diverse group of reef life, about one-half to three-quarters are carnivores, leaving only a minority as herbivores. There are in fact more herbivorous fish on a reef than in some other ecosystems, but even here fish are primarily a carnivorous group. With fish, the pyramid appears to be upside-down.

One answer to this emphasises the very highly integrated nature of reef life. You cannot just take the fish in isolation. By themselves, the fish do form an upside-down pyramid, but it is a small pyramid that has its place within the whole, larger pyramid of the reef—and that one is right-side-up with its apex pointing upwards.

Where then are the herbivores? Some fish are herbivorous of course and of these probably the most significant are the parrot fish and surgeon fish. The parrot fish have evolved specialised beak-like mouths which rasp algae off the coral rock. They may feed alone, in groups, or in large schools which migrate along a reef, feeding frantically and leaving rocks criss-crossed with fresh white scars. Added to these are the coral-feeders, trigger fish, file fish and the attractive butterfly fish. These eat coral polyps, but since the polyps contain a lot of symbiotic algae they too must be counted as partly herbivores.

It is on the sea bed where probably the most important grazers of the reef are found. The sea urchins are the most visible as they rasp their way over the rock. The long-spined *Diadema*, with its light and shade sensors which allow it to aim its spines towards objects overhead, is the most important grazer and has species in the Caribbean and in the Indo-Pacific regions. The pencil urchins also feed on algae and several species eat sea grass as well. Some herbivorous crabs and molluscs will always be found in fairly small numbers and probably most of the major animal groups contain some plant-eating members. But still there seem to be too few to fill a traditional herbivore level.

Recycling and Microbes

To begin to find the answer to the problem of the lack of herbivores we can examine exactly what it is that the animals on the floor of the reef do eat. Here there is a surprise for those used to the traditional chain of simple relationships of plant-to-herbivore-to-carnivore. Most of the reef-dwellers are suspension-feeders, detritus-feeders and filter-feeders. The surprise lies in the fact that we know there is very little suspended food in the tropical oceanic water or in this water when it reaches a coral reef. There is nowhere nearly enough to support the almost infinite variety and large volume of such animals on the coral reef. The suspended and detrital particles, then, must come from the reef itself.

This suspended food appears to be one of the keys

(*Above right*) Sea urchins, such as this *Diadema*, are often the most conspicuous herbivores on the reef. They graze by scraping algae from the rock with their mouths, which are located on the underside of the body. *Diadema* has been known to feed on coral occasionally.

(*Right*) One of the most important groups of herbivorous fish are the surgeon fishes. This species is *Acanthurus lineatus*, which lives in shallow areas of the reef. They are named because of small, sharp barbs which they can extend from near the base of their tail fin and use for defence.

(*Far right*) The slate-pencil urchin is another mainly herbivorous animal. This one, *Heterocentrotus mammillatus*, is seen mostly in crevices during daylight, where it apparently wedges itself with its thick, triangular spines. At night, it can be seen foraging.

to the jigsaw of the life on the reef. It is derived from several sources, but whether directly or indirectly, it comes ultimately from plant life. First there is the portion of fragmented plants themselves; dead, dying and even dissolving plant matter that has ceased to photosynthesise. A second source comes from faecal matter and the particles resulting from the disintegration of dead animals. This is essentially recycled matter. A third part is from the mucus of corals and other coelenterates. This is organic matter exuded into the water by the coral polyp, but this excess production is only made possible in the quantities that exist because of the photosynthesis of the symbiotic algae in the polyps. In a sense, algae are responsible for this. Fourthly, there is that part of the zooplankton composed of the larvae of animals. Again, when this plankton comes from a coelenterate with symbiotic algae, its production in large quantities is made possible partly by the energy supplied to the polyps by the algae. The larvae in other words are, in terms of energy at least, partly a result of the action of the plants which are captive in their parents' bodies. A large proportion of reef plankton is from such animals. To this group of zooplankton can be added a group called *demersal* plankton, creatures which live in crevices in the reef during daylight and rise up into the water column at night. This group originates on the reef rather than arriving from the open ocean, and is another part of the suspended food which is available to filter-feeding and suspension-feeding animals.

So there are many sources of suspended matter. But the story has one vital still-missing link whose activities enable all these sources to exist. This link is provided by bacteria. These micro-organisms decompose and recycle everything which dies on the reef; plants which are free, plants captive in corals, and all animal life and its products. The result is that there is a remarkably high density of bacteria on the surfaces of rock, in cracks in the reef and on dead matter. They themselves are particles and, singly or in clumps, they provide particulate food for anything from worms to corals. The reef would simply not work without bacteria. They are the principal agents of recycling organic matter and they function in a way so efficient and rapid that they can be said

to direct the ecosystem. It has long been known that the typical reef is a living system which lacks large external supplies of food, depending instead on rapid and efficient recycling of nutrients and organic matter. This is performed by the bacteria so well that little of value to the reef is leaked back into the ocean.

Therefore, despite the shortage of herbivores, it appears that we do have all the links in the food chains and all the levels in the pyramid. It is just that the second food level, that of the herbivores, is rather complicated. It is still there, however. Put simply, plants are either eaten directly or are broken down into particles which feed the suspension-feeders, in ways aided by the bacteria. We must not forget those particles from animals which are fuelled to a large degree directly by captive algae. Once we have this secondary production in the form of suspension-feeders, herbivores and growths of bacteria, then the third level, that of carnivores, is relatively straightforward again. At every stage, and in every food chain, there are many feedbacks and interconnections, however, and there is much that we still need to learn.

Hiding for Protection

It is difficult at first sight to see where the necessary plant basis of the reef lies. Similarly it is not always clear exactly where all the different kinds of animals are. We can readily see several dozen if not hundreds of kinds of coral, soft coral and gorgonian, and scores of different fish at any one time. Otherwise, as we swim a metre or two above the reef, we see various assorted starfish and sea urchins, sea cucumbers on the sand and a collection of molluscs and crustaceans. But, from this distance, we do not see anything like the variety to justify the statement that the reef is the richest ecosystem in all the oceans. For this we need a closer look.

The fact is that a very large proportion of the species on the reef are *cryptic*, i.e. they live inside some kind of shelter for much of their lives. When it is remembered that about two-thirds or more of the swarm of fishes hovering above are carnivores— and carnivores furthermore which often do not mind what sort of animal they eat—then a concealed

The crown-of-thorns starfish, *Acanthaster planci*, is a well-known coral-feeder. It everts its stomach over a coral colony to digest the food and then absorbs the products before moving on. Entire coral colonies and large areas of reef are killed when large numbers of these animals appear.

The triton shell, *Charonia tritonis*, is one of the largest gastropod molluscs in the world and is a predator of the crown-of-thorns starfish. *C. tritonis* is Indo-Pacific, and a very similar species, *C. variegata*, is found on Atlantic reefs.

The starfish *Fromia* is a carnivore, taking small animals such as molluscs into its stomach. Just as the majority of sea urchins are herbivores, so most starfish are carnivores.

The murex shell, *Murex ramosa* (*left*), was found feeding on an oyster (*right*). When turned over here, the murex animal withdrew into the shell, sealing the aperture with its tough operculum. It has been suggested that the spiny nature of the murex shell deters predators.

This Caribbean bristle worm, *Hermodice carunculata*, is a bottom-dwelling animal which feeds on coral polyps and, as in this case, on polyps of soft zoanthid corals. Each animal can eat about 1 square centimetre an hour, but they are rarely found in densities great enough to cause much damage.

The racoon butterfly fish, a species of *Chaetodon*, feeds entirely on coral polyps. The butterfly fish are one of relatively few groups which eat coral.

This fish, called *Choerodon*, uses its strong jaws to overturn pieces of coral rock and expose beneath the small invertebrate animals which form its prey.

life style becomes easy to understand. Evolutionary pressures—the survival of those which are hidden and a rather short life for those which are not—have ensured that the concealed way of life is immensely popular.

Such a life style does indeed bring shelter and protection to the hidden animal, but it may also mean that it has a very restricted mobility. If it cannot go out and search for food, then it must rely on food coming to it. This, in its most reliable form, is small particles suspended in the water currents. The animals can simply develop methods of trapping the suspended material and stay largely concealed.

It is not surprising then, that suspension-feeders are one of the main groups of reef animals. The necessity of staying concealed, and the abundance of food put into suspension by processes of breakdown and decay, both fit together perfectly and have given rise to this major category of reef life.

The variety of these animals is extraordinarily diverse, as is their manner of catching food. There are those which freely move about within their protected area, and those which are fixed in one position for all their adult life. Small crabs are a good example of the first group and the tube worms well represent the second. Animals which bore into rock span the two groups.

A coral head provides shelter for all these groups. Within the branches of a bushy coral, such as *Pocillopora* or *Acropora*, there will be a high density and variety of animals which obtain protection from large predators. Small crabs and molluscs in particular, and many brittle stars, reside there, all scavengers or suspension-feeders, eating anything which opportunity provides. On the branches will be bumps like galls. Here is where other species of crab have settled permanently, allowing the coral skeleton to grow around them until only a small hole allows the exchange of water to the crab. These have given up all movement for the added safety of the limestone walls, as they cannot leave their chamber. This resembles the way of life of the barnacles, which are also crustaceans, except that with the barnacles the stony walls are modified plates of the crustacean body itself and are not produced by the coral. Several barnacles may exist in the coral head, their limbs modified into 'feathers' which rhythmically sweep the water. Some species have obtained what must be nearly the ultimate in protection. They live in the centre of the large polyps of corals, such as *Goniopora*. They have a case like other barnacles but are also surrounded at all times by the stinging polyps and tentacles of the coral animal. The barnacle's sweepers are clearly immune to the stings

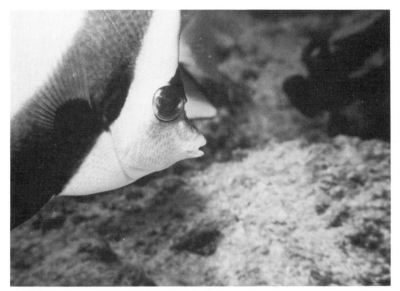

The long-fin banner fish, *Heniochus acuminatus*, is a butterfly fish with a more varied carnivorous diet. The elongated snout of this and many of its relatives enables them to take a range of invertebrates from crevices.

The puffer fish, *Arothron*, includes large sponges in its diet, leaving characteristic bite patterns. Like most fish, it has a mouth or beak well suited to its task.

(*Left*) The French angel fish, *Pomacanthus paru*, of the Atlantic reefs feeds on a varied diet of small animals. The most available are small worms and molluscs, with some crustaceans.

(*Below*) A top carnivore, the barracuda, *Sphyraena barracuda*, feeds on fish which are mostly themselves carnivores. These fish may be seen singly or in schools.

(*Right*) Both the clams, *Tridacna*, and the coral, *Lobophyllia*, in which they are embedded, are partly suspension-feeders. The clams pump water through their bodies and filter out particles while the corals rely on capturing the particles with tentacles. Like the corals, the clams contain symbiotic algae and both derive nutritional benefit from this direct plant source.

Ascidians, or sea squirts, pump water through their bodies to filter out nutritious particles. Some, such as the small group (*below right*), thrive in very silty conditions while the solitary stalked one, *Polycarpa* (*far right*), lives in clear waters.

of its host, but what is most intriguing is how the barnacle, as a larva, first gets to that position, avoiding the tentacles whose main function is to catch zooplankton.

A much underestimated group is the worms. There are, literally, thousands of kinds, falling into several unrelated categories. There are the nematodes, tiny detritus-feeders which play a vital role in the recycling of dead matter. Nemertines are thin and long with very elastic bodies. Sipunculids tunnel into and under corals; these are more stubby, fatter worms. Then there are the polychaetes, or bristle worms—the worms which have legs. Many of these also live under coral and in crevices, but the most

The remarkable suspension-feeding mollusc, *Vermetus maximus*, has a shell which is modified into a tube cemented to rock. This view into the tube shows the head and tentacles. The animal casts a web of sticky threads into the current and then, when the food particles have stuck, it withdraws the web.

Some of the ocean's largest fish are filter-feeders. The manta ray swims near the surface around reefs, scooping large volumes of planktonic animals into its open mouth. *Manta birostris* may weigh 2 tonnes.

conspicuous group of bristle worms is probably that which lives in tubes sunk into the living corals. These polychaetes have, in the course of adopting their tube-dwelling mode of existence, largely lost their limbs, except for those that now hold the body securely in the tube and except for their crowns. Their crowns are the whorls of colour extended from the coral or rock. They are feathery structures which are very sensitive to movement and which flick back into the tube at the smallest hint of danger. These crowns serve two main metabolic functions of food capture and gas exchange. They act as gills while they are out in the water fishing for particulate food.

Two large groups of animals carry their protection with them. The crustaceans and molluscs have approached this in totally different ways, the first forming an exoskeleton which is arranged to provide jointed limbs, the second growing a shell which is no help at all in the movement of the animal. But for both groups the hard case provides protection. The complicated arrangement of the crustacean skeleton means that it cannot grow with the animal and so must be discarded when it becomes too small, whereas the relatively simple mollusc shell can be expanded when necessary, simply by adding limestone to the aperture end.

Given that the hard cases of these two groups provide protection, it is surprising perhaps that so many of them still hide. Both groups have members which remain almost permanently in concealed places or which move about under sand. The reason is that, whatever the armour, there is always something bigger which can evolve a means of penetrating it. It does not matter to the 4-metre-long nurse shark, as it searches for sand-dwelling molluscs, how thick the shell is; it still cracks them with ease. In this case, the layer of sand does not help much either. But it is a protection against the other animals which it encounters most frequently. A crevice-dwelling mollusc or crab will usually only encounter another species which is small enough to be in the same crevice and against these their armour is usually sufficient.

Much smaller animals than the nurse shark have evolved mouths or limbs for penetrating skeletons and shells. Many of these are found amongst the crabs and molluscs themselves. The claws of some crabs are used to crack open mollusc shells. Two ways of doing this have been well recorded: the first is to crack off the spire of the shell bit by bit until the body of the mollusc is reached from behind. If the mollusc shell is too tough or is unsuitably shaped for this, the crab may chose to 'peel' the shell from the aperture end. Some molluscs, in their turn, can drill holes through other shells in order to reach the flesh. Gastropods, for example, can get at bivalves in this way. Frequently, dead shells washed up on beaches are found to have a neat hold drilled in them, which gives away the nature of their demise. Many fish also have mouths which are hard and strong enough to crunch through such protection.

So, despite many forms of protection, and this includes camouflage and poisons, armour, spines and speed, a very large number of reef animals also hide, by occupying existing crevices or by making tunnels of their own in such numbers that the honeycombed corals may eventually collapse. This largely concealed world within the reef is an extensive, thriving and vital one.

On the surface of the reef the animals are, quite literally, exposed to everything. The surface, as we have seen, is the domain of the coelenterates: corals and their octocoral relatives, the soft corals and sea fans.

The acres of exposed corals, soft corals and sea fans generally seem to be an undesirable food source for most of the hovering mass of fish. The amount of predation on these coelenterates is remarkably small and the percentage of all species which feed on them is tiny. If it was higher than it is, then perhaps the reefs of the world as we know them would not exist. The reason why soft corals are rarely eaten is due in many cases to the fact that they contain very high levels of toxic substances. Some will damage the skin of your hand if you touch them. It requires a remarkable digestive system to handle these, but, as always in this marine world, some do exist. The poached-egg cowrie eats them for example.

Nobody really seems to know why the stony corals are not preyed upon more than they are. They certainly have a reasonably good nutritional content as several fish survive entirely on them. It is true that

(*Left*) Suspension-feeding sabellid worms in the Caribbean reach a length of 30 centimetres and have feathery fans which trap food and act as gills to supply oxygen. Because the fans are so important to the animals, they have a very fast withdrawal reflex when disturbed, contracting into the protective tube.

(*Top right*) The twin whorls of filaments are all that is visible of these serpulid worms as their entire tube is sunk within the living coral colony. Their whorls are also well-protected, when withdrawn, by a kind of trap door which seals off the entrance.

(*Top far right*) The need for protection is why the hermit crab carries a discarded mollusc shell. Most crabs have their own armour but this group has unprotected abdomens. This crab has taken a shell from a dead spider conch.

(*Right*) The large nurse shark is not a fish predator, like its better-known relatives, but feeds largely on sand-dwelling crustaceans and molluscs when it is not lying asleep on the sand.

they have stinging cells and, while the little darts are too weak to hurt us, our hands may be quite different in this respect to the sensitive lining of a fish's mouth. The answer may simply be that fish and other animals are stung if they try to eat them. A hint that maybe animals would find corals palatable if they could only get at them is that the polyps of most corals are tightly retracted during daylight. Even species which do not contain algae do this, so this is not only a response to optimise the light. In the light, fish can see and might well consume waving tentacles if they could. But, when tightly deflated and retracted into their cup-shaped depression on the stony surface, the tissue is certainly much harder to get at.

While they might not be eaten much, corals are affected by the grazing action of herbivores. Parrot fish and sea urchins especially rasp their algal food off the rock and, in so doing, they destroy very large numbers of juvenile corals. But studies of this effect have shown that this grazing happens at a level which is of optimum benefit to the corals as a whole. In fact, both more grazing and less grazing than the natural levels results in detrimental effects to the corals. It is easy to see how more grazing is harmful; more juveniles are damaged and destroyed. If there is too little grazing, however, then there is an increased rate of plant growth. Algae grows so much faster than corals that the corals become swamped and smothered under a thick layer of plants, so in this way also corals suffer. This has been proven by experimentally changing the numbers of grazers on patches of reef and it shows how finely balanced and integrated the life of the reef is and how any interference can be harmful to the system.

To prevent themselves being eaten is thus a major preoccupation of the majority of the thousands of different species which live on the reef. Armour, poison, camouflage and a hidden way of life are very common amongst reef-dwellers which is why we do not see the greater part of the reef's diversity in just a glance. It is undoubtedly true that the major cause of death amongst reef-dwelling species is to become prey to another. That is why so many young are produced by each pair of parents and any young which are just that little bit better at avoiding such

a fate might pass on its secret of success to its own offspring. This is the mechanism of evolution and the constant pressures of survival on creatures is one of the things which has resulted in the so many different species found today. Equally however, the pressure to develop is on for the hunter as much as it is for the hunted. No matter what lifestyle a species now has, its hunters have had equal time and equal chance to develop too, so that the art of hunting has taken many paths, with some species becoming very specialised in it. In the labyrinthine world of tunnels and crevices for example, where soft-bodied and vulnerable creatures hide, specialised carnivores amongst the crustaceans, worms and molluscs roam as well, living their whole adult lives there and continually stalking their prey.

For some animals, being eaten in their adult stage is not so much of a problem and the surface-dwelling coelenterates appear to be firmly in this group, whether because they get protection from their skeletons, because of stinging cells or other reasons. Although they are food for some specialised animals, they are not preyed upon too heavily. They thrive in great abundance in the open. Their algal cells provide the major plant source of the reef as well. These large and highly visible components of this closely-linked world of animals and plants live over large areas of the reef, from the topmost part at the low-tide mark to depths where the sunlight just fails to illuminate sufficiently.

Yet many things have an important influence over which species of coral (or soft coral or sea fan) lives where; which species live in deep or shallow water, in turbid water or only in the most clear. The distribution of each species on the reef and the limits to where they can grow are subject to quite a wide range of controlling factors, which complicate the simpler considerations of eating or being eaten. There is the hostility of the underwater climate for example and factors of competition between species, even between those which do not feed on each other. Many things like this structure the life of the reef and have caused it to evolve to its present spectacular state. You can readily see that certain corals live in certain depths and places, for example, and so now we can turn to some other aspects of their struggle for survival.

6. THE SURVIVAL PROBLEM

IT HAS BEEN more than a couple of hundred years since the first naturalists marvelled at the coral reef, and it has been nearly a hundred and fifty years since men first studied reefs in a way which we, today, would term scientific. But just in case we think of those men in those times at all patronisingly, think no further than Charles Darwin, whose book in 1842 on the natural history of coral reefs made a quantum jump in man's knowledge of and approach to such things, which has scarcely been equalled by one man since. No single person has succeeded so strikingly in advancing our understanding of nature as he did, although many famous names have appeared who have vastly increased our knowledge in later years. His book on coral reefs, arguably more original and providing a bigger conceptual leap than even his more famous later works on evolution, marks the start of what we choose to term the modern science of reefs.

It was appropriate, and no coincidence, that the same man should develop the sciences both of coral reefs and of biological evolution. In the latter, he showed exhaustively that living things were under pressure for survival from all sides—from the environment and from other types of animals and plants—and that they changed or became extinct as a result.

In the sea, these same pressures apply, and this is vividly true on the coral reef with its vast array of species. Here, one of the main objectives of research for a hundred years has been to determine how environmental factors affect life on the reef, and how competition between species for food and for space resolves itself and affects the whole community.

While many able and now well-known people advanced knowledge of these things, they were limited in what they could achieve, not by their own vision but by technology. They were almost entirely confined to the reef flat where they could go on foot. This environment, as we saw in an earlier chapter, is subjected to heat and to drying out. Many reef flats have a good and varied cover of living things, but many others are remarkably poor. The deeper areas, which later proved to be where the richest, most diverse and concentrated life lies, remained the *Mare Incognitum* as it was termed, for a long time. This persisted until the middle of this century, when, in terms of reef ecology, another quantum leap forward was made possible. This was due to the invention of a widely available aqualung by Gagnan and Cousteau, and it brought the rich reef slopes within reach of almost everyone. The first scientific information of reefs obtained with the use of this device appeared in the 1950s and the early trickle of information has now risen to a flood.

From this information, it is clear that the reef is a world of especially intense struggle. We saw in the last chapter that one major struggle that animals face is finding food and preventing themselves from becoming food for others. Other struggles, such as that against the physical environment and that for space in which to live, are just as important in

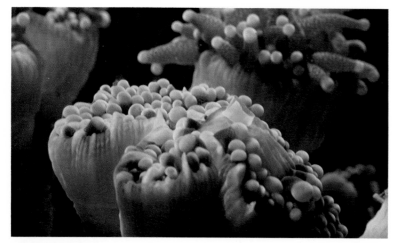

This long-tentacled coral, *Euphyllia*, survives in relatively silted parts of the coral reef. This is something which few coral species can manage and so it faces much less competition from other species than it would do in more crowded areas. A barnacle which has solved its own survival problem can be seen protruding from the nearest polyp. The barnacle is protected by the polyp's tentacles.

The coral species, *Stylophora pistillata*, lives over a wide depth range and shows different growth forms under different conditions. There is a slender, fragile colony (*above left*) from a deep area, where there is little water movement and little light, while the other (*left*) is a stout form which was fashioned by strong waves in the shallows.

The delicate vase is a colony of the coral, *Turbinaria*, over 1 metre in diameter. Such growths are found only where the water movement is never violent. A little water movement is desirable, however, as it helps keep the surfaces free from silt.

The coral on the right, called *Euphyllia ancora*, is attacking the one on the left. These corals were placed in an aquarium about 12 centimetres apart and left for about 10 days. During this time, the *Euphyllia* detected the presence of the other (a species of *Goniopora*) and developed special sweeper tentacles to deal with it. These are longer and narrower than normal tentacles and are loaded with stronger stinging cells. These grew only on the side nearest to the target coral and their role is simply to kill it—which they did.

determining the pattern of life on the reef, especially for animals which are permanently attached to the bottom as corals are.

Responding to the Environment

In shallow water the action of the waves is at its fiercest. A single coral colony in this area may receive a blow from many kilograms every few seconds, so it is obvious that physical strength is necessary to live here. Brain corals and many rounded and flattened shapes survive in these areas and it is not surprising that thin leafy corals are never found in such conditions.

What is surprising is that several branched species do occur. These are tough, but not as tough as the encrusting or rounded species. Their strategy appears to be to deflect a large part of each onslaught of water rather than stand up to it. The most spectacular way in which this is done is by that largest member of all branching corals, the Caribbean elkhorn. Its massive branches are strong, but clearly not overly so, as they can be readily snapped off by anchors of boats or by clumsy divers. Yet it grows mainly in the shallows. What it does is to produce branches which orientate themselves into the direction of the prevailing waves. This way, each tip faces into the impact, presenting a relatively small area to the force. Branches could presumably not remain attached if they grew broadside on. This species is called *Acropora palmata* and a smaller close relation, *Acropora palifera*, grows the same way in shallow Indo-Pacific waters.

In these shallow regions, the action of waves is the most important control over which species can grow where. These *Acropora* species can tolerate strong physical forces due to their adaptation of shape and so they are very important reef-builders on shallow parts of the reef.

There is an advantage in having some water movement, provided it is not too strong, as it keeps the surfaces of the corals swept clear of sediment. If the water is very still, particles fall out of suspension and smother everything which is attached to the bottom. Corals differ considerably in how well they can cope with, and remove, a rain of silt. In a calm

lagoon, where a lot of silt builds up on the bottom, the species that will be found are those capable of shedding layers of silt and preventing themselves from becoming smothered. Relatively few can do this well, so in such areas there will be fewer and often different species to those found on reef slopes where there is an appreciable current.

Another most important physical control over corals is that of light. The amount of light declines as greater and greater depths are reached. It is clearly the case that some corals require a lot of light, while others can grow just as well under very much dimmer conditions. By the time a depth of 30 metres is reached, many species can no longer exist, while leafy species actually increase. It is true that the absence of strong wave action at these depths has a lot to do with this but, equally, it seems that these leafy corals manage to do better under low light conditions than do boulder-shaped corals. The plates of these colonies are held outwards from the reef in a way designed to catch as much as possible of the light. They are very rarely held out at the very best angle for light interception, however, as this would be in many cases perfectly horizontal which is also the best angle for intercepting falling sediment. So leafy corals are most commonly seen at a sort of compromise angle; flat enough to receive most light, but sloping sufficiently to let the sediment slide off or be pushed off by the coral with a minimum of effort.

You notice also at about 20 or 30 metres deep that the average size of the corals becomes smaller. This too is probably the result of the reduced amount of light here. Presumably, corals need to expend energy in depositing their often substantial limestone skeletons, although whether this involves a lot or a little of the total amount of energy at their disposal is one more of those unsolved problems of coral science. But it is probably very significant that the leafy shape, which so many of the deep-water species have, is a shape which requires less deposition of limestone than, say, a boulder or branching structure.

Thus the fall-off in light with depth, the strong water movement in the shallows and the rain of sediment in sheltered parts of the reef are all important aspects of the marine climate which affect corals, and all the other life of the reef too. On the reef flats, as we have seen, heat and drying-out are equally important climatic conditions which the life there has to face, but these are not important in the deeper areas. Where climatic extremes exist, they all increase the struggle of the corals.

Each of the many hundreds of species responds to the marine climate in its own way. The number of species seems enormous and, because many corals take on different shapes in different conditions, the number of coral species seems even greater than it really is. Take, for example, the common branching species, *Stylophora pistillata*, shown on page 70. Each picture shows the same species from the same reef, taken within a hundred metres of the other. The one in the shallows is stubby and tough and it can withstand the battering from large waves. It has far more physical strength than the spindly one from deeper, sheltered water. Such differences are common in several bushy species. (For a long time, in fact, it was thought that these were two different species and it was only when a detailed study was made and a series of colony shapes in between these two was found that it was realised just how varied a single species can be.) Corals are said to show a high degree of plasticity in this respect, which all adds to the impression of an infinite variety of life on the reef.

Important though strong waves, silt and reduced light are, these physical influences are not always the most important things which affect corals or the other life. Over a lot of the reef, physical conditions may in fact be fairly benign. Here, there is just the right amount of water movement to keep sediment from building up, but waves are not fierce enough to cause physical stress and there is plenty of light. In such regions, which on many reefs encompass the areas between depths of 3 and 30 metres, the majority of species would prefer to live—if they could. But here lies their problem. Because so many want to live here, the competition between them becomes intense. In the next section we see some of the extraordinary array of methods that corals and other species have of helping themselves in their struggle for life and for living space, and some of the ways in which their interactions with other animals assist them in finding some refuge from the competition.

Corals at War

Over a lot of the coral reef, where the physical climate is, in general, benign to the reef life, everything would like to live. As a result, competition there is the fiercest of any area. The fact that not all species do live here means that many have been edged out, into deeper water perhaps, or into turbid areas where they face much less competition for space. Most species, however, have either centred their existence on this area, or at least overlap with it to a considerable degree. To survive here, species have developed a number of different qualities and each species must have one and preferably several aces up its sleeve if it is to live here with any degree of success.

Some species produce large quantities of young. Their strategy is to flood the area indiscriminately so that, hopefully, some young will survive. Others produce fewer young, and thus reduce their own energy wastage, but may endow the young with special qualities which help them to survive, such as a good ability to hunt out favourable spots on which to settle. Other species hardly seem to breed at all, but rely on the fact that their fragile skeletons are easily broken by waves and scattered about. Then the fragments re-attach and grow into large colonies themselves. Other species may simply be rapid-growers, finding their safety in fast growth and large size. Others fight for space.

The simple animals that make up the colonies of corals and soft corals have developed several mechanisms which enable them to increase their size at the expense of others or to defend their own living space. As you look at them, corals do not appear to be doing anything very much, except to grow more slowly than you can see. They appear to be static, apart from those whose tentacles have expanded and are waving in the currents. All look frozen in a still life. But we look on it with our sense of time, not theirs. In fact, a war is going on where species compete in many ways for survival. To us it is in slow motion, where a lightning strike by an aggressor may take many months! But it is none the less vigorous for all that. For the coral polyps there is a fight for survival as literally as there is on an African

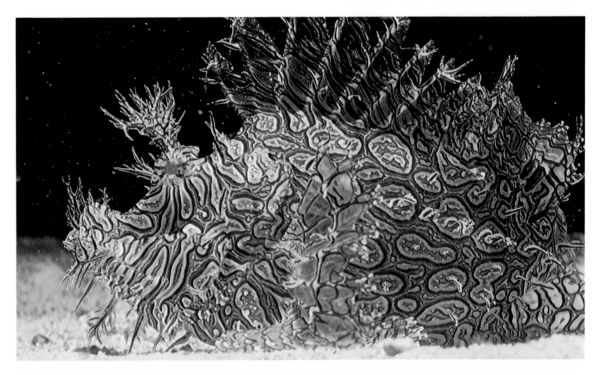

(*Above*) The soft coral, *Efflatounaria* (*left*), has leap-frogged a patch of algae by pushing out a tendril. This attached itself onto the rock on the right where it has grown into another colony. Eventually the connecting tendril will break. This method is an effective way of expanding and avoiding competitors.

(*Right*) Nudibranchs or sea slugs are usually very well camouflaged or brilliantly conspicuous. Colourful ones, such as this, are avoided by predators since they are known to be poisonous.

(*Left*) Colouration and pattern is all important on a coral reef and manifests in several ways. The poisonous lion fish, *Pterois* (*bottom*), uses its colours as a warning display. Predators know to leave this fluttering animal alone. The rare green *Rhinopias* (*top*) is well camouflaged and waits for unsuspecting prey fish to come within range of its mouth.

75

savannah, although with the difference that the participants cannot flee but must remain rooted to the spot of their initial attachment. Corals have several ways in which they can attack others.

The ordinary tentacles of corals contain stinging cells and, in a few cases, these can be used to keep a small area around them clear of other animals, especially other corals. A large number of them, however, do much better than this. These develop especially long tentacles which are known as *sweeper tentacles*. These may be ten or twenty times longer than the normal tentacles and develop when the coral polyp detects, presumably in a chemical way, the presence of another coral nearby. These may take a week or two to grow, but considering the slow rate at which the neighbouring coral is closing in on it, this is usually quite fast enough. The new sweeper tentacles are endowed with a particularly high concentration of particularly strong stinging cells. When these have grown, they wave about in the water in the direction of the target and, when they touch it, they stick onto it and kill it. The attacker thus defends its space and no longer runs the risk of being overgrown from this source.

There is another, much faster mechanism which is employed by many coral species. This is to send out digestive filaments from its own body cavity. The attacker simply detects the presence of the target, which may be food or a potential danger, opens up a hole in its own body wall and sends out these filaments. This may be completed within a couple of hours of detecting the prey. Within a couple more, the prey is completely digested away. At first sight, this seems to be a better mechanism than the sweeper tentacles, but it lacks the range of the tentacles as the filaments can only reach out for 1 or 2 centimetres. When both mechanisms can be used by the same species, the filaments reach only a half to a tenth of the distance that can be covered by the sweeper tentacles.

The battle is not only between the corals. Soft corals, too, have an equally strong interest in survival and they have a different set of strong cards to help them achieve it. This group seems to use poisons as its main weapon. The bodies of many species are filled with a particularly unpleasant group of chemicals, called *terpines*, which seep out into the surrounding water, killing nearby organisms, especially corals. The process of leaching out these chemicals is probably continuous. The effect at first on a coral growing 20 or 30 centimetres away may be to slow its growth and distort or distress it, which is accompanied by loss of colour and discharge of mucus by the target. As the soft coral grows closer towards the affected coral, the dose of chemical which the coral receives becomes stronger and stronger until, eventually, the target is killed.

Not all soft corals can do this and some have poisons which are stronger than others. Sometimes, as well, stony corals can beat the soft corals using their own mechanisms of attack. It has not been proved, but it may be that some stony corals can also secrete toxins which help them to compete against other species. Certainly, some of the distances which these coelenterates can cast their lethal effects are very impressive, considering the small size of their polyps.

The result of a conflict between two particular species can sometimes be fairly consistent. In other words, a sort of hierarchy may be seen. It is not a simple or straightforward matter, however. If we look only at one of the mechanisms of competition, e.g. the one involving the extrusion of digestive filaments, then species A may always kill species B when the two meet. This is usually very consistent on its own. But where another mechanism is also involved, e.g. sweeper tentacles, then B may kill A if B is the species with the longer tentacles and the longer reach. So the question of which species usually beats which others is very complex because many checks and balances occur. A species strong in one mechanism may be less strong in others.

Added to this are the environmental factors. To have long-reaching tentacles may be all very well in calm water, but they are quite useless across a strong current. If the species having these long tentacles has no other cards to play, then it may only be able to survive in conditions which are calm enough to allow it to deploy them. Likewise, the poisons secreted by soft corals have a greater range in still conditions where the poison may concentrate in the immediate vicinity. In fact, where there is a very gentle current

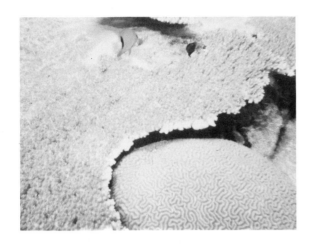

(*Top*) The results of coral conflicts take many forms. Here a brain coral, *Ctenella*, has been using an unknown means of preventing a table coral from overgrowing it. Within range of the brain coral, the polyps of the table coral are killed.

(*Above*) A different form of aggression is shown by the coral *Lobophyllia* (*right*). It detected the presence of its rival within a few hours and threw outwards a bundle of filaments from its own digestive cavity. The filaments cover the rival coral and simply digest it away. The filaments are then withdrawn. This method of attack is very rapid but has a fairly short range.

always in one direction, the effects of the poison may be seen more than 1 metre down-current of the soft coral. In turbulent water, however, the poisons are instantly dispersed and their effectiveness is lost.

The speed at which a coral or soft coral can grow is

also an important factor to consider when determining just how competitive it may be. Fast growth can be a very strong card for the species concerned as it may simply allow the colony to grow out of trouble. This ability is shown to perfection by the soft coral *Efflatounaria* which puts out 'runners', just like a plant. These can leap-frog over hostile and unsuitable areas, attach, and then develop daughter colonies before the runners, or stolons, break to isolate the new colony.

In the Caribbean, there are several species which have a slow growth and which remain very small at all times. These, all other things being equal, seem vulnerable and liable to be overgrown. But other things are not equal, as these are the strongest of all in the Caribbean in terms of being able to defend their space by filaments and tentacles, so their slow growth is balanced out.

In the Indo-Pacific, there are some species which are both aggressive and have fast growth. The combination of both things provides a nearly unbeatable mixture and we would expect these species to be very successful. They often are, and vast areas may be thoroughly dominated by them. Examples are some of the species of *Acropora*. But these too have their limitations and cannot grow everywhere. Something always precludes these species from complete domination; a fragile skeleton preventing it from living in shallow, turbulent water perhaps; some limitation imposed by the amount of light it must receive; or an increasing vulnerability to predation or erosion when it becomes too abundant. Checks and balances apply to these species too, despite their possession of two strong cards. There are, after all, dozens of cards in the pack and no one species has them all.

The challenge facing any coral colony or any other type of organism on the reef comes from several fronts. The marine climate and the organism's ability to cope with it sets the boundaries on where it can live. Then, having begun to grow within the kind of area which is not too severe for it, its challenge comes from other species which similarly strive to live in the same area. Being eaten by something else is the first and most drastic problem, which is why an astonishing two-thirds of reef species are toxic. In addition,

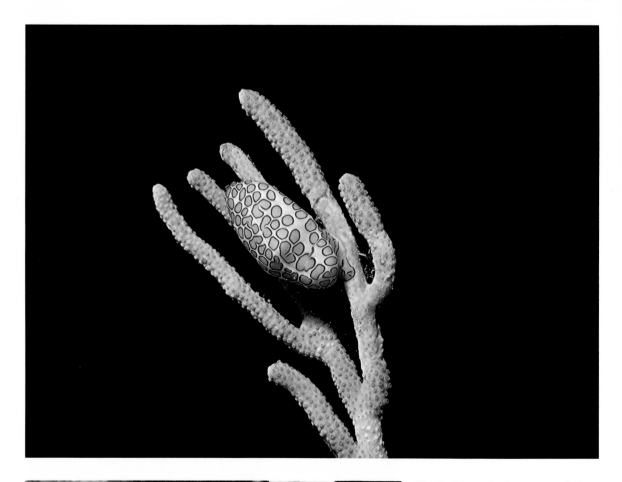

The Caribbean flamingo tongue, *Cyphoma*, stands out clearly on sea fans which are its principle habitat and source of food. Being highly visible seems to be of little disadvantage to it.

A classic association is that between the clown fish, *Amphiprion*, and the sea anemones of a group called *Stoichactis*. The anemone may benefit a little from food caught by the fish, but the fish finds protection amongst the stinging tentacles for itself and for its eggs, which are laid under a fold of the anemone.

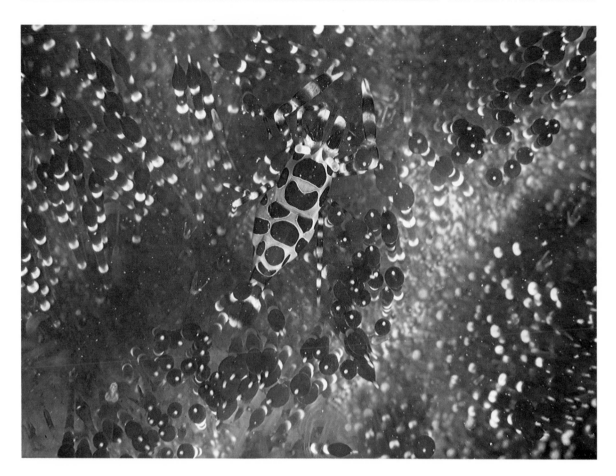

Crustaceans are unsurpassed at camouflage. The little red shrimp (*top*) blends in beautifully with the body of its host—a sea urchin. The shrimp (*bottom*) is on the arm of a feather star. The shrimp is black with yellow tips to its appendages, just like the spines on the feather star's arms. These may feed on food caught by their hosts and so the association may border on parasitism.

79

The cleaner fish escapes being eaten by its distinctive coloured stripes and by its characteristic twisting movements. It then picks parasites off larger fish, in this case an angel fish, to the advantage of both.

The sleek remora, *Echenius*, finds protection, free transport and probably food by attaching itself to a large fish by the sucker on its head. It is quite common for one to detach itself from a passing shark and attach itself to a diver.

many different kinds have some sort of stony armour and the majority of species also hide. Those that develop some means of gaining a competitive edge in their environment may do well. Others may develop some feature which allows them to live at deeper or shallower depths and avoid much of the competition. Many species find an advantage in living in a close association with another, quite different, species.

Close Alliances

Nothing illustrates better the mutual benefits gained when two widely different organisms live together in close association than the symbiotic zooxanthellae and coelenterates. But many even more surprising associations are continuously being found which illustrate both the interdependence of reef life and the axiom 'survival of the fittest'. Many species have found that a life in close association with another species can bring increased benefit to it and many cases can be seen in which this association has pro-

gressed to such a degree that, today, the species can only live in that association.

A lot of degrees of association exist in which quite different animals, or animals and plants, share a habitat or depend in some way on each other. Usually, a *commensal* relationship means that one party benefits from close association with the other, but that the other neither benefits nor is harmed. In a *symbiosis*, both partners benefit and neither may be able to live independently. But the distinctions between these two are often blurred. *Parasitism* is when one party benefits at the expense of the other; this category may blur into some forms of commensalism and, in some cases, is also interchangable with simple predation. The boundaries are not clear cut and we use these words only to help describe what we think is happening; often we are not even clear about that.

Many associations on a coral reef are now classics of zoology. These include the banded clown fish which lives in sea anemones. The fish are not stung by the anemone and gain protection from it. They do not seem able to live except in the anemone. From the anemone's side, there may be little advantage in the arrangement, although the fish have been seen to feed the anemone by bringing food to it.

Crustaceans show many associations. On sand, there is the shrimp which shares a burrow with a goby. Other shrimps clean edible particles off the skin or scales of a wide range of animals, even from the teeth of willing moray eels. Some smaller ones have gone further and now live around the mouths of animals, such as starfish and their relatives, and even inside the mouths or on the tracts that carry food to the mouth. These steal the food caught by their unwilling host, so this association borders on parasitism. Several of the species which feed like this can only live on one species of host. Sometimes they have grown to look like a part of the host, camouflaging their own outline for their own protection. Many nudibranchs, the colourful sea slugs, show this art to perfection. Several live on particular sea fans or hydroids and look exactly like a part of the sea fan which they are eating, both in colour and in shape, even to the extent that their gills are shaped like polyps.

Perhaps the most fascinating association of the coral reef is that developed by the cleaner fish. One or a small group of these wrasse, called *Labroides*, sets up a cleaner station where larger fish queue up and have their parasites picked off their scales, their gills and even from their mouths by the cleaner fish, to the obvious advantage of both. The distinctive blue and black stripes of the cleaner fish are clearly recognised by their large, carnivorous customers at the station and ensures the cleaners' survival as they feed. However, the cleaner station is made more remarkable yet by the existence of a false cleaner fish. This is very similarly shaped and coloured, and bears the unlikely name of the sabre-toothed blenny. The fish waiting to be cleaned are fooled by it and allow the blenny access. But the blenny is a mimic and then demonstrates its unsavoury practice of biting a chunk out of the other fish, often from its gills, and making it flee. Every opportunity to gain is used on the coral reef.

Some of the largest carnivorous fish of all, the sharks, will attract other commensal fish. A quivering group of pilot fish may float just in front of the shark's nose, bow-wave riding just as dolphins do in front of a ship. And even less effort is expended in getting around by the remora, which attaches itself to the body of a shark by means of a sucker on its head. As well as obtaining free transport, these fish find protection from potential predators as well. Some confused remoras can mistake a wet-suited diver for their more usual host and can be almost impossible to scare away as they repeatedly attach themselves to your legs or arms.

All these life styles are designed to let the species concerned get more food and more protection and to have a greater chance of finding a mate. In short, species have evolved these close alliances to secure a better chance of solving their own survival problems and continuing their line. Sometimes the consequences extend beyond benefiting that species alone.

A good example of this is found in the way in which reefs of the eastern Pacific resist devastation from the coral-eating crown-of-thorns starfish. The corals which primarily build these reefs are of the bushy group called *Pocillopora*. In their branches live small commensal crabs. If a crown-of-thorns climbs onto one of the corals, the crabs immediately nip its tube feet, repelling the predator. Thus it saves its coral host and its own home from being killed. Not only that, but it saves the entire reef and allows it to continue growing as well, since these corals are the main builders here.

The consequences of these small crabs are enormous. They show how the downfall of one small part of the reef's life may result in the collapse of something very much larger; in this case the reef itself. It shows too how potentially fragile the reef is. It is teeming with life, but consider this: the riotous life that we see reflects not so much a robust and strong web of life, but more one which is frantically and rapidly working in a desperate attempt to keep going. This is an ecosystem which is easy to destroy.

In his life, Darwin brought together the two notions of the development of a coral reef on one hand and the consequences of competition for survival on the other. You can see both happening when you dive on a reef.

Night falls rapidly on tropical reefs. The last rays of sunlight refracted down by a wave crest illuminate a pattern of activity on the reef which is changing to its night-time mode.

The swift bluefin trevally, *Caranx melampygus*, feeds well during the confusing illumination at sunset, picking off fish which have lost their school or which have not yet hidden in their night-time spot on the reef.

Tightly-packed schools of fish seem to crowd closer as dusk falls. There is safety in numbers for these fish and their schooling instinct means that they are a difficult target for predators.

About half a metre long, this young white-tip shark is a species of *Carcharhinus* which is occasionally found resting on the bottom. It will reach a length of 2 metres when fully grown and is a top predator on the reef.

7. DAILY RHYTHMS

FOR many reasons, one of the most impressive times of all to see the reef is during the hour before sunset. This is the hour when the tempo of life soars until there is, wherever you look, a frenzy of activity. Much of this movement is the feeding of the fish—feeding of the more violent, predatory kind. Other activity is caused by fish moving singly or in schools from their daytime positions to nighttime sites of greater safety. Then, looking beyond the simple increase of movement, it is possible to see a more profound change beginning to take place in the life on the reef and around each coral head. Different species appear and others disappear and a transformation happens to the surface of the coral itself. In essence, life on the reef changes to its nocturnal mode.

Nightfall

On those isolated offshore reefs where oceanic waters are close by and where fish are always numerous, it becomes obvious when it is feeding time on the reef. Schools of glinting *Caranx* and *Pompano* slice into clouds of millions of tiny fish whose instinct keeps them tightly bound together by invisible bonds of self-protection. The clouds lurch this way and that, each fish turning in synchrony with all the others. But, trained by millenia of evolution, the formation as a whole never breaks or sends the fish scattering. Some individuals do lose their place and are short-lived thereafter. Mackerel, tuna, barracuda or other swift hunters scoop up these strays with just a small deflection of their body and jaw. The errant fish never passes on its genes again, so that only those keeping refuge in their own school can breed and thus maintain their collective schooling instinct.

Above and all around, the chasing and the fleeing continue without a break; the carnivores must eat and the pursued must elude them. To be in the midst of the swirl and flashing scales is an awesome experience, particularly when a dozen or so reef sharks join in the fray. When seen during the periods of relative calm in most of the daylight hours, these, the white-tip and black-tip sharks of the genus *Carcharhinus*, cruise slowly by and rarely hang around when they determine that there is no future for them in a diver. At feeding time, however, they change their mood and loose any semblance of sedateness. With backs arched up and pectoral fins dipped down, they lurch about in a way assured to rivet your attention. In sideways lunges, they snatch at fish, tear them with their jaws and, convulsively swallowing them, continue their swerving progress along the reef. Some at this stage will be sure to focus their attention on any divers about. A prod or two with a shark-stick deters most, which then return to easier prey. Sometimes one or two may be more persistent, in which case it might be prudent to leave the water with great care, back-to-back and keeping them well in view. However, even in waters heavily populated with sharks, it is fortunately fairly rare for sharks to turn unprovoked on divers. Occasionally they do so, but it is usually not difficult to avoid a potentially dangerous situation and there are times of the day and states of the tide when it is best not to dive.

This activity builds up in a remarkable way as the sun dips towards the horizon. Then, as twilight deepens, there comes a stage when most of the activity ceases. Fish which are vulnerable to predators seem to vanish and the predators which remain are harder pressed to find their food. For 20 minutes or so the reef life is relatively still, spanning a period when light falls about a thousand-fold, from dim to very dim indeed. This is termed the 'quiet period'.

What has happened is that many of the daytime active fish have left the water column, seeking refuge for the night, while most of the night-time active fish have not yet emerged. There is not a gradual replacement of the daytime population by the night-time one, but instead there is a gap of about 20 minutes when neither inhabit the water over the reef. This is because this is a particularly dangerous time for fish to be out and about. It appears to be fairly quiet, but predation is intense for those not in hiding. The predators make good use of the confusing light.

There is a good explanation for this. The light receiving structures in the eyes of daytime fish begin to fail in these low light intensities, leaving this group vulnerable. But the dimming light is still too strong for the best efficiency of the much more sensitive light receptors in the nocturnal fish's eyes, so that these do not work well either, leaving the nocturnal group vulnerable too. It has been shown that fish which are artificially released into the water over the reef during this dangerous period do not have a high chance of survival. Although the vision of the predators may suffer too, this is a time when the prey species are at the greater disadvantage. So most make sure they are hidden before the quiet period begins and those fish, such as schools of grunts, which move to different areas of the reef for the night, do so before their failing vision can endanger them.

Many fish stay in holes and crevices through the night and show a greatly reduced level of activity or none at all. They simply go to sleep. Some do so to such an extent that a gentle handling of them does not produce any reaction at all beyond a sleepy stirring—quite a different situation from their day-time behaviour. If they were not well-concealed they could not possibly survive the nocturnal predators. Of the fish which go to sleep, perhaps the parrot fish are the most remarkable. These build a cocoon around themselves every night, made from mucus secreted from their bodies. In this they sleep, lying on coral or on a patch of sand. The cocoon provides protection as they lie asleep, possibly by disguising the edible contents inside the package from a passing predator, such as a moray, or even by repelling it with distasteful chemicals. Other fish, such as grunts, mute their strong colours through the night. Their vivid bands which are so necessary in their social and schooling behaviour during the day become a liability at night when these behaviour patterns temporarily cease. A more blotchy, indistinct camouflage pattern would serve them better and at night this is exactly what they have.

These strategies for hiding are necessary because of the powerful vision that many nocturnal carnivores have. In this they can be compared with their aerial counterparts, such as owls and other night-time birds of prey, whose sensitive eyes are better known to most of us. It is amongst the fish, however, but not necessarily those of the coral reef, that the most sensitive eyes in the natural world are found. Some very deep-water fish for example have eyes capable of detecting just a few quanta of light— about the smallest quantity of light that can exist and still be there. Such extreme sensitivity may not be necessary in the clear shallow waters on a coral reef, even on a moonless night, but adequate vision is possessed by many hunters. Many come up to the reef from greater depths at night to feed, returning to deep water in the morning. Others come in from far offshore, going out to sea again at first light.

However, acute vision is far from being the only sense which enables such hunters to exploit the reef. The vision of sharks for example is not particularly good, but several species step up their predatory activities in the dark. These species use a combination of several senses, including smell, vibrations picked up by organs located down the lateral lines of their bodies and, sometimes, even electrical sensors in their noses. All help them to seek out their prey amongst the life of the reef at night.

(*Left*) At the start of the 'quiet period', fish find their night-time places of safety. Parrot fish find a crevice and make a mucous sleeping bag in which to spend the night.

(*Right*) Unfurled tentacles of a branch of the bushy *Dendrophyllia* coral at night. This species contains no symbiotic algae but it too is open only at night.

(*Left*) Night-time transformation of the corals. The coral *Lobophyllia* is in its contracted state (*left*) as we usually see it. When it senses that daylight has gone, it unfurls its zooplankton-catching tentacles (*right*), which remain out till dawn.

The corals also behave quite differently during the period of darkness. In darkest crevices first, then on the exposed surfaces, the coral polyps unfurl as dusk descends, sending out their crowns of tentacles. Small transparent tentacles may emerge from the valleys of a brain coral, while opaque and pigmented ones come from a boulder of green-brown cups. In over-hangs, each cup of orange *Tubastraea* sends out a bunch of vivid yellow tentacles to hang in the water, twitching sometimes, fishing for zooplankton. No photosynthesis occurs for the next 12 hours or so in any of the corals here, even in those which contain symbiotic algae. No carbohydrates are fixed by the algae which instead must draw on the reserves which were built up over daylight hours. Somehow the coral polyps can sense that light has gone and that it is time for catching animal food instead.

How polyps sense this is not known. In that major-ity of reef corals which contain algae, some chemical changes which accompany the slowing and stopping of photosynthesis may inform the polyp that night has arrived. But this night-time expansion also happens in those which do not have algae in their tissues. Neither the orange *Tubastraea* nor its green-tentacled relative *Dendrophyllia* contain algae and so might seem to have less need to respond to the daily cycle, but these too open up all over the reef at about this time. Their response to light is very fast indeed, and is certainly no slower than the response of their symbiotic neighbours. If you shine a torch on their expanded polyps they close up in a matter of a few seconds. This response to light limits the length of time when corals can catch zooplankton to the hours of darkness only, which reduces the length of feeding time for non-symbiotic kinds by about half. But de-spite this, it provides some advantages to the polyps which outweigh their loss of food. Quite likely, it avoids having its tentacles eaten, which are pro-tected instead within their stony cups during the time when predators could see them.

Faint markings resembling tiny, opaque dots on the otherwise transparent tissue may be visible along the length of the tentacles. These are the batteries of stinging cells, many newly-made to replace those discharged the night before. When a sting has been used, it cannot be reloaded. Instead, new ones are

formed deeper in the tissue and moved out to fill a vacant site when one appears so that a polyp keeps its efficiency as high as possible.

The early part of the night is the best time for the polyps to be out since zooplankton is what they seek. Now is the time when a group of minute animals called *demersal plankton* rise. This includes a wide range of species and particularly small crustaceans, but they all have in common the tendency to hide on the bottom in crevices and in branches of the corals themselves during daylight and to rise up-wards through the water as night falls. To do this, the later ones must pass through a gauntlet of sting-ing tentacles from corals, although many can avoid this by leaving just before the polyps unfurl. Never-theless, the fact that they do migrate in this way, preferring the risk of being caught by corals to re-maining in the water column all the time, suggests that this way of life is still safer than the hazards of being eaten in the day by fish. Despite their noctur-nal habits, however, many still fall prey to the noc-turnal reef-dwellers.

On many coral boulders there is now a spread of ten to fifty feathery arms, all curving upwards from a central point to form a bowl shape. Reds, blues and oranges are their commonest colours and each may be a hand's span or more across. Sometimes one or two of these animals will flap their arms and swim, clumsily compared to some sea creatures but still with apparent purpose, to a different perch. These are the feather stars, or crinoids, an ancient group of animals belonging to the echinoderm, or starfish and sea urchin group. Their arms make an efficient net for plankton trapping and the food caught in them is passed down to an upward-facing mouth. So efficient are these nets that many are unwilling hosts to several scroungers, tiny crustaceans and worms, which steal the food before it reaches the feather star's mouth but avoid being caught themselves. These very fragile creatures are not at all a rare sight in daylight either, but it is mainly at night that they unfold their arms and appear from their daytime crevices in great numbers. Through the day they are more commonly seen as a tangle of arms enmeshed in a sea fan's branches, awaiting the dusk before un-curling. Then, over a period of about an hour, you

With the night come scores of feather stars, or crinoids. They climb atop a coral or a sea fan and spread out their arms into the current to trap drifting plankton.

One of the most bizarre animals on the reef at night is the basket star, whose multiple-branching arms trap drifting plankton in a similar manner to its relative the feather star.

will see at least a doubling and more likely a ten-fold increase in the numbers out on the reef.

An even greater web of arms in a sea fan may indicate a basket star, a more bizarre, multibranching relative of the feather star. These behave in the same way, but a close examination of their tiny disklike bodies at the centre shows a downward-facing mouth, indicating that they are more closely related to the brittle stars which are a more modern cousin. They have parted from the bottom-crawling, agile ways of other brittle stars, and, while retaining many aspects of their basic, ancestral body anatomy, in-cluding a downward-facing mouth, have joined the feather stars in a more sedentary way of life. They too have developed a web of plankton-trapping arms.

All these animals prefer high points on the reef, sitting at night at least on a protruding lump of coral if not on a sea fan a metre or two above the floor of the reef. This enables them to spread their nets above the slow-moving boundary layer of water on the floor up into a faster flow where they more frequently encounter the plankton that provides their food.

All through the night the pace of life continues, much of it on a miniature scale and in close contact.

For many species, the senses of touch and scent are the main ways of detecting the world about them. Hunters come out of the sand and sense the chemicals in the water which give away the presence of their prey. Many of the most beautiful molluscs in the sea do this, then close upon their prey with remarkable speed. Tun shells, olives and volutes envelop their food in their mantles, finishing off the prey with a bite. The cone shell kills its prey in a more spectacular manner and from a slightly greater distance. It too detects prey using scent, then flings out a lance-tipped proboscis, stabbing the prey and injecting venom. So quick is this, that even fish are occasionally caught and the poison from a few of the dozens of species can kill an unwary person.

On most nights, the reef is never completely dark. Phosphorescent plankton, which are quite invisible during the day, sparkle clearly. On moonlit nights, if clouds permit, light from the full moon may penetrate sufficiently for us to see as deep as 20 metres without torches. The cycle of bright moonlight happens every month and many events occur in synchrony with the lunar cycle. At fixed points in the cycle, many species of animals, especially of corals, release their clouds of eggs or larvae into the water. The precise nature of the trigger for these events is not yet determined, but it may well be connected to the light or to that other related aspect of the moon's phases: the tides. Several other factors seem to be important, too, such as water temperature, but it seems that, although the trigger for such spawning is fairly complex, it correlates well with the lunar cycle, even if only indirectly.

For most of us, the shallow parts of the reef near the shore are those which are the most accessible at night. On the reef flats and shallows, many different animals come out from hiding. Here, molluscs especially wait until dark as well, when they emerge from crevices to forage. The colourfully-shelled cowries are amongst the commonest molluscs on the reef flat at this time, with several species living on the algal ridge itself. Most are omnivorous, eating plant and animal alike, whatever they chance upon. Sponges, worms and tiny crustaceans, as well as algae, all form part of the diet of many species of cowrie. The tiger cowrie, *Cypraea tigris*, the gold ring cowrie, *Cypraea*

(*Top*) The wing oyster of the Caribbean, *Pteria colymbus*, lives firmly attached to gorgonians. Elevated above the slow boundary layer, it intercepts more food than if it were attached to rock. The period of day when this food is most abundant is near dusk when demersal plankton rise from the reef and into the higher water column.

(*Above*) A pair of flatworms mating. Many reproductive events are tied to cyclical physical events, such as the daily period of darkness or the lunar cycle. Spawning often occurs simultaneously amongst many quite unrelated species, all taking advantage of unknown events at these times.

annulatus, and the many others which emerge at night are *photophobic* animals, i.e. they dislike light. The reasons for this are twofold: firstly, by remaining in a crevice during the direct heat and ultra-violet radiation of the sun they avoid much of the stressful forces that these bring; the second reason is the same as that which causes their relatives in deeper water to emerge only at night—they can hunt with less chance of being hunted. For them it is safer this way. They are fleshy animals and so are a ready source of food themselves for many other species, especially fish which rely mostly on their eyes. They still face a threat, however, from each other and from large crustaceans, but not such a severe threat as they would face in the day.

Daybreak

As the light of dawn hardens the outline of the shadowy reef, the changes which took place at dusk the previous evening slowly reverse themselves. There is another 'quiet period' between the disappearance of the nocturnal fish and the reappearance of the daytime hordes. Before you really notice it, the tentacles of the coral polyps have vanished, withdrawn into their skeletons. On the bubble coral, *Plerogyra*, large, pale blue-brown bubbles of tissue which are located at the base of the tentacles are inflated with water by the polyps. As the tentacles turn inwards, these are pulled out to take their place. They contain particularly large amounts of symbiotic algae, and this foretells the main trend of the reef at this moment: the transition once again to photosynthesis. By the time the sun's rays are clearly visible in the water, most corals have withdrawn into their skeletons. Those which remain are the species which are out all the time, except when touched. *Euphyllia* stays out and so too does *Goniopora* with its long polyps capped with tiny tentacles. All day long these feed. Whatever causes the polyps of all other species to retract does not concern these species.

Throughout the day, many other coral colonies may extend their tentacles sporadically, if only partially, in response to an unseen stimulus. It may be that a substance in the water, such as an amino acid, has passed over the coral which recognises it as food. Corals can detect one part in a billion of these chemicals and respond by going into a characteristic feeding posture, with tentacles expanded and mouths open. Generally, however, the polyps are closed as far as feeding on zooplankton is concerned.

The early sun flooding through the water makes

Polyps of the very similar corals, *Plerogyra* and *Physogyra*, are expanded at night like many others (*top*). At dawn, however, as they retract their tentacles, little spheres attached to the base of each tentacle are pulled out and inflated with water. This causes the entire surface of the coral to be covered with bubbles, seen (*above*) on an entire, small colony. The bubble tissue is filled with symbiotic algae so this mechanism improves the ability of the coral to photosynthesise.

this a most enchanting time to dive. The awakening parrot fish shake off their mucus shields and continue where they stopped the previous dusk, rasping at the algal-covered rocks and corals. Their discarded sleeping bags last just a few minutes before they disintegrate and disappear. Another day begins.

8. SAND CYCLES

FROM THE MOMENT that they settle and begin to grow, coral colonies on all parts of the reef are attacked and eroded continuously from above and within. The white sand of a coral beach is proof of this. It has its sparkling appearance because it is pure limestone sand, which has been made from ground-up corals and other organisms from the reef. There may be flecks of colour in it, fragments of mollusc shell for example, but it is basically pure white. Where beaches have sand of any other colour it is because ground-up rocks and minerals from land nearby and not only from a reef are involved.

The coral sand, and coral rubble which is its earlier state, is made continuously in two main ways: by the breakage of fragile colonies, caused mostly by waves, and by the tunnelling and boring activities of animals and plants. Both these things act in conjunction, so that the combined assault continually reduces the largest colonies, firstly to rubble-sized fragments and eventually to sand.

It is now known, however, that this sand—the result of the destruction of the reef and reef organisms—is in fact also one of the key building components of the reef. This paradoxical situation comes about because sand is continuously reconsolidated into rock and the result of this rebuilding is harder rock than the skeletons of the corals once were.

Before this can happen, sand must be trapped. Intact corals, and anything that forms pockets in the reef, make important sand traps. The corals provide a framework which holds and stabilises the sand when it is formed and prevents it from being continuously shifted along by water movement. Then, when the sand is well impacted into holes, a process of cementing begins, the sand particles which originated from the limestone skeletons of corals go full circle to be turned back into solid limestone again, but this time of course, not into the intricate shapes that they had before. Most simply, this happens when any encrusting organism, but especially red algae, grows over the pocket of sand, sealing it inside. Chemical and physical changes then occur which eventually weld the particles together, cementing them into a solid block of reef. Some estimates suggest that a reef may grow about a millimetre per year. As individual corals can grow ten or a hundred times faster, this suggests that most of the coral which grows on the reef is eroded down to begin the sand cycle.

It is true, of course, that many coral colonies reach considerable size and remain more or less intact when they die. You can see boulders over 10 metres across, supporting millions of polyps, on almost any part of the reef slope. Quite obviously, these provide a substantial part of the reef rock just as they are. But if it is possible to distinguish between the contribution of corals as a whole to the process of reef formation in this way and their contribution as a framework which traps sand and actually produces sand, then the latter is probably more important. Of course, the type of coral is critical. Delicate, branching corals, for example, turn into sand very easily

The importance of sand is evident from the sheer quantity of it made on any coral reef. In an atoll lagoon, sand is piled up to form a beach and it even makes whole islands. It is all white limestone: the ground-down skeletons of coral reef organisms.

Close-up of a sieved portion from a bucket of 'coral' sand, showing some of its major components. The tip of an urchin spine (*top left*) points at the disk of a foram skeleton. Three or four whole micro-molluscs and fragments of larger mollusc shells are present, with a crustacean skeleton and bryozoan and algal fragments. Most of the fragments are coral skeleton.

Corals such as this delicately branching *Seriatopora* are very readily fragmented and quickly made into sand.

Only a little more sturdy are several species of *Acropora*, such as this *A. formosa*. Fragments of these also provide a large portion of the sand.

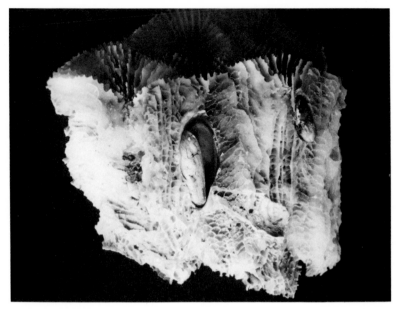

A large quantity of all coral skeletons become worn, etched and turned into sand by boring and tunnelling animals. Here, a small boulder coral has been broken open to reveal two tunnelling bivalve molluscs. The skeleton of this coral is fairly porous and light in substance, so the bivalves can tunnel through with ease.

while solid boulders of coral are probably more likely to become incorporated into the reef just as they are.

Making Sand

The bioeroders—that is, the tunnelling, etching and chiselling forms of life—are therefore a critical part of the reef even if, by their very nature, they are largely unseen. Sponges and bivalve molluscs riddle many reefs and are probably the most important groups of animals to destroy corals from within. Many if not most of these groups secrete acids to aid their excavations. This is a particularly effective way of eroding limestone since this rock has an alkaline nature so is very readily dissolved by even a mild acid. Sponges and other organisms which have no mechanical moving parts must rely entirely on dissolving the rock away if they are to live inside it. Some molluscs supplement this acid-etching process with mechanical methods of tunnelling and some do without acids altogether. Bivalves are well suited to this as they are simply hinged in such a way that they rasp at the rock with their shells.

Plants are also responsible for a certain amount of bioerosion. These, especially filamentous green algae, also work their way in, sometimes using the minute naturally-existing pores in corals. They generally remain in the surface layer of the coral or lump of rock into which they are tunnelling as they still need light. That they can penetrate at all is due in large part to the slightly translucent nature of the limestone which allows light through to a very small extent. The main algae which lives in the limestone of living corals is *Ostreobium*, and it is usually pigment from this plant which is responsible for the very persistent green colour seen in some coral specimens even after they have been thoroughly cleaned and bleached. These living algae may be found as much as a centimetre or two below the surface, although a few millimetres seems more common. They may not weaken the coral very much and in fact it seems likely that they may even contribute to its nutrition in a similar way to the symbiotic algae within the polyps. But, however much these algae may erode living coral heads, the wider range of algae which bore into dead ones are more destructive.

One very important but not at all inconspicuous group of sand-makers are the parrot fish. These get their names from their parrot-like mouths which are designed for crunching coral tips or rasping living matter off rock. Many species of these fish feed on algae growing on dead corals and other rock. In the

95

process, a lot of the rock is taken in along with its food. It is thoroughly ground up by the fish's digestive system and the rock particles are actually a necessary part of the process, causing the plant tissue to be properly digested. The sand is then discharged in a fine cloud when everything of nutritive value has been digested from it. This fine silt amounts to many tonnes per year on every hectare of reef. Parrot fish are major contributors to the sand-making process and hence to the reef generally.

Not all sand comes from corals. There are other stony coelenterates such as blue coral, *Heliopora*, and organ-pipe coral, *Tubipora*, which are related but not true corals. Calcareous algae are also very important. Red algae are the most visibly dominant, especially in shallow water, but the most important one of all in some areas is the green algae called *Halimeda*.

This is an unmistakable plant, consisting of chains of little hard segments; green kidney-shaped disks which have a diameter of a few millimetres to a centimetre or more, depending on which of the dozens of species it is. It occurs, often profusely, in both the Caribbean and Indo-Pacific areas. The plant deposits limestone within its disks and each chain may add an entire disk every day. Very often, one plant consists of many branching chains so that it daily produces dozens of new disks. Although the disks are hard, the connections between them are fragile so that water movement or disturbance from browsing and grazing animals breaks them off quite easily. The disks soon become part of the sand and, because of their shape they are an easily identifiable part, at least until they become ground down to minute grains. Some sand patches, especially in sheltered areas behind reef flats and in lagoons, consist almost entirely of dead *Halimeda* segments in various stages of disintegration, but almost always with a layer of whole disks on top. The living plants will be conspicuous near such a patch, perhaps immediately above it on a steep reef slope where their growth may festoon the side. Great streams of detached disks continually flow down from such a wall to form hillocks at its base. On seaward reefs, however, abundant growths of *Halimeda* are usually less common because of greater disturbance and grazing activities, although the dead disks may be almost as

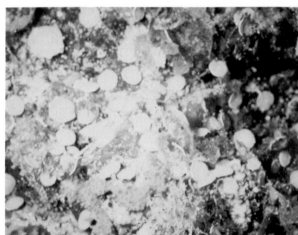

(*Top*) Green disks of the plant *Halimeda* are 95 per cent stone. Each chain can grow a disk per day, which very soon dies and breaks off, becoming a major source of sand.

(*Above*) Round disks of protozoan animals in the group Foraminifera. These are about 5 millimetres across and because of their large numbers the skeletons of many species make a very sizeable contribution to the sand.

(*Right*) Walls of gullies may be festooned with *Halimeda*, whose disks pile up at the base. In cases like this, the covering of the floor may be entirely *Halimeda* sand.

abundant. Sometimes only small tufts are visible. The plants will be growing just as fast but the greater disturbance breaks off and scatters the disks before the plants can reach a large size.

Molluscs play a part in rubble and sand production too. Apart from the actions of many in turning corals into sand by their boring activity, their own shells eventually make a direct contribution to the sand. When the soft body of the mollusc dies it leaves no trace, but its shell becomes ground down into fragments in a similar way to all other stony materials on the reef. It too is made of limestone, although it also contains other chemicals, including several which give colour to the outer layer. In ad-

dition there is a very diverse and prolific group of molluscs, often conveniently termed the micro-molluscs, which are only slightly bigger than grains of sand themselves, even when adult. These may be found everywhere on the reef, but especially in the sand, becoming a part of it when they die.

There is another very important group of animals which adds to the sand in an even greater way. These are the Foraminifera, or forams for short. They are protozoan animals which range in size from smaller than a millimetre to a couple of centimetres across. These make a sort of skeletal case, which, once again, in most cases is limestone. Some are planktonic forms whose cases fall downwards after death to form a

97

very substantial part of the sediment in deep ocean areas, where the sediment may be termed *Globigerina ooze* after the main group of species. On reefs, they are enormously abundant on and in the sand where, in some patches, they are the main and apparently sometimes the sole component. Other species are attached to rocky substrates. Amongst these are several kinds which have adopted a colonial mode of life, to form small encrusting sheets with an important role in binding together sand and rubble. In terms of what they do, encrusting forams are similar to encrusting red algae, a likeness which is increased by the fact that some of them, such as the important Caribbean *Gypsina*, contain photosynthetic algae.

Whatever the origins of the sand, all the time an important grading and sorting process is taking place. Small, light particles can be shifted more easily than heavier lumps, so where there are gradients of current there are usually gradients of sand size too. For example, water pumped by waves across a reef flat will move or pick up a considerable load of particles on its way. When the deeper area beyond is reached, the water velocity immediately slows down and the sediment begins to drop out of suspension in a sequence. Larger particles fall first and the finest silt settles out last and furthest away. Where a lot is continuously dumped there will be a smothering thickness of sand or silt, preventing growth of corals and other attached animals and plants. But this does not mean that these sandy areas are lifeless.

Using Sand

The great expanses of sand behind most patch reefs and in most lagoons are far from lifeless. Usually, the species living here are those adapted exclusively to a soft substrate existence, so that they only occur here and are rarely seen on the hard substrate of the reef slope. Brownish-purple patches can cover wide areas in depths which have sufficient illumination, the patches being a film of a type of algae which has the capability of fixing nitrogen. Additionally, masses of diatoms, and small tufts and patches of larger green and red algae occur, all adding a lot of organic matter to the sand. This provides food for a lot of animal life in the sand.

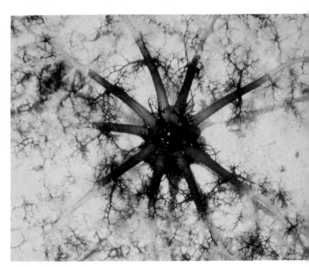

(*Top*) Major inhabitants of the sand are the sea cucumbers. They ingest vast quantities of sand, digest the organic content from it and excrete the sand again.

(*Above*) A burrowing sea cucumber catches food on its unusual, extended arms which then transfer it to the mouth. When disturbed, this creature, *Neothyonidium magnum*, can withdraw into its burrow.

(*Right*) Sand is rich in molluscs. One of the largest Indo-Pacific sand-dwellers is this helmet shell, *Cassis cornuta*. This is one of the few which live on the surface of the sand; most mollusc species live just beneath the surface.

Micro-molluscs and forams feed on the algae, as do worms, larger molluscs and many burrowing urchins and other echinoderms. Most conspicuous of these are the sea cucumbers, some a metre long or more, others very fat. They feed by ingesting large volumes of the sand, extracting anything of any food value and ejecting the sand itself. Feeding by animals causes continual mixing of the surface layers. Conical mounds show the presence of many burrowers and tracks along the surface give away the presence of the most diverse group of animals here, the molluscs. The marlinspike, called *Terebra*, and the olives, cones and volutes are amongst those that have a life

beneath the sand, hunting each other or the many small worms and crustaceans. Some corals may be found on soft substrate too, especially adapted forms which are not attached to the substrate in adult life.

These include species from several coral families whose other members are typical rock-dwellers. Most sandy and muddy substrate corals are Indo-Pacific, but live only in relatively small portions of this area. Attractive colonies of the coral *Moseleya* and *Catalaphyllia* live on mud and fine sand in the Far Eastern/ Australian area, while *Trachyphyllia* lives on similar substrates spread over a larger area across the Indian Ocean as well. Some of the corals attach themselves

99

initially to small but solid pieces of mollusc shell or rubble, but they soon outgrow this temporary substrate. One small type, called *Heteropsammia*, settles initially on a small dead mollusc shell which it slowly engulfs as it grows, but before it completely covers it the shell is occupied by a particular species of sipunculid worm which then lives with the coral. As the coral grows, the worm maintains a tube inside the base of the coral and keeps open one main entrance and several pores. The coral is regularly moved small distances by the worm. Because all specimens of this coral contain this worm, and apparently only a single species of each is involved, this association

(*Top left*) A thicket of *Acropora* coral on a sandy plain gives shelter to a school of needle or razor fish, *Aeoliscus strigatus*.

(*Left*) A common inhabitant of sand and coral rubble is *Polyphyllia talpina*, one of the free-living mushroom corals seen here with tentacles extended.

(*Above*) The lizard fish is a common sight on sand, where it props itself up on its pectoral fins. It feeds on small fish.

may well be a kind of symbiosis, although its exact nature is still a mystery.

The most widespread and abundant corals of the sandy substrates are the mushroom corals, whose commonest members are the group *Fungia*. These are large, solitary polyps—though there are colonial relatives too—which live on coarser substrates than do the other unattached corals. In fact, they span all types of substrate from solid reef through rubble to coarse sand. They grow initially on mushroom-shaped stalks attached to rock or rubble, but later the flat disk on top breaks off to live an independent existence, leaving the stalk and moving away. By

virtue of their numbers in areas such as lagoons, they are a very important part of the whole reef. When they die they leave behind relatively durable skeletons which may provide the only lumps of solid substrate on the sand for a wide range of other reef-dwelling corals, so that oases of corals appear, surrounded by sand.

It is in the sand that the enchanting commensal pairs of goby and shrimp are found. There are many species of both. The fish guards a tunnel, resting on the sand by the entrance. Then, every minute or so, a shrimp appears, acting like a tiny bulldozer, shovelling out a pile of sand before it with its claws. The

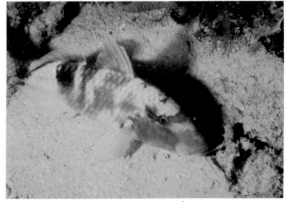

(*Above*) The apparently lifeless sand is actually filled with concealed animals, excavating burrows and chambers. The rate of this activity can be seen from this experiment where a film of dark quartz sand was spread over the white limestone sand. This photograph, taken a day later, shows how much burrowing and mixing of the surface layers takes place.

(*Right*) Another sand-dweller is the flathead, *Platycephalus*. This one feeds on small fish which approach within range of its mouth as it lies well concealed on or just under the sand.

(*Top left*) One brightly-coloured species of burrowing fish is *Nemateleotris magnificus*, which lives in small groups in a tunnel. Its tall dorsal spine flicks characteristically when it is in the open. Beside the entrance to this tunnel are a collection of filter-feeding tunicates.

(*Left*) *Parupeneus macronemus*, a member of the goat fish group, is found commonly over sand in shallow areas. It has two long feelers positioned near its mouth with which it probes the sand, feeling for its prey of small invertebrates.

tunnel appears to need endless maintenance, judging by the continued digging by the shrimp. The goby's part of the arrangement is to provide the food and to give an early warning of danger to the poorly-sighted shrimp by beating its tail, causing vibrations which are detected by the shrimp's antennae.

Recycling

In general, the area of sand is usually much greater than the area of hard reef which does much to supply it. A large part of the lagoons of atolls, and extensive areas behind or to leeward of reef flats, are covered by sand which comes from several sources to provide the foundation of tomorrow's reef. If we can make a jump in the time scale, we can see that the sand becomes aged and compressed by the weight of more above it. It is slowly transformed from the form called *aragonite*, which is deposited by corals and many algae, to a more durable form called *calcite*. Both are forms of calcium carbonate which comes under the label of limestone (not sandstone, which is a quite different mineral).

The processes of rock formation appear to continue on the beach. A lot of beach and island rock are remnants of past reefs made when the sea was higher but, in the region of the high-tide level, new rock appears to be constructed as well. Slabs of rock, inclined downwards towards the sea, are the most usual configuration. The level at which they are made is often that where the water table is positioned, so that chemical changes to the sand by fresh water are one possible cause. Also, slabs of similar shape may be seen, composed of sand grains mixed with a black organic material made from micro-organisms. The slabs have a top layer of a living green-black sheet of micro-organisms and the whole slab has the texture of still-soft cement. Living processes here also help to build upon the coral reef.

There are forms of reef life which lay down other rock containing different minerals, especially silicates, but the vast majority of the reef-dwellers which leave any trace at all deposit calcium carbonate, especially in the aragonite form. This mineral is readily available to the organisms as the tropical sea has as much as it can hold of it in

Beach rock in the making. Patches on the coarse coral sand of thicker, clay-like material show one of the processes of reef-rock formation at work. The patch slopes down towards the sea, as do many rock slabs, and has a film of living algae and micro-organisms on top of a black mixture of dead matter mixed with sand. It seems as though this eventually hardens by chemical processes to form durable rock.

solution. The high degree of solution is maintained because a lot of the finest sand or silt continually redissolves.

So there is a cycle here too; the reef organisms extract calcium carbonate from the water to deposit in the form of skeletons of their own particular sort. By erosion, it is turned into rubble, sand and then into finer and finer particles. Then some redissolves again to complete this cycle. The sand which does not redissolve is accreted into solid rock, the reef of the next generation of corals. Much of this too is later tunnelled and eroded into sand, forming a side loop of the sand cycle.

In several parts of the reef, however, whether it be an atoll, patch or barrier reef, the accretion of solid rock is faster than its erosion by waves and bioeroders combined and so the reef grows. The areas where this happens may not necessarily be the areas where corals grow fastest and most luxuriantly, but may be beside them, or down-current of them, where the sand produced by the corals finally ends up.

The actions of waves and of boring animals and plants, so destructive at first sight, are in fact a necessary, integrated part of the formation of the reef. They help to provide an important part of any reef and one which is home to a large quantity of many species of life.

9. LABYRINTHS IN THE REEF

A CAVE entrance underwater is a tempting sight. The darkness inside cloaks everything and so at first you cannot tell whether it is filled with life or fairly barren, or even whether it is large or small. Caves are common in many types of coral reef, especially in those which have steep slopes. There may be both simple caverns or complicated networks of interlocking chambers and passages.

A colony of sea fans may guard the entrance like a curtain, swaying as trigger fish bend them back to leave on a feeding trip. A different world is contained inside, one that is quite alien to a human being. So it is always with a tingle of anticipation that you enter.

If it is a proper cave rather than just a notch cut into an overhanging bit of reef, it stretches perhaps a few metres in all directions. It probably has a sandy floor, level with the lip of the entrance. It is wise, until your eyes become adapted to the dark, to float near the central point so not to brush against any stinging sedentary animals, or worse, animals with teeth or poisonous fins.

Cave Dwellers

As the gloom appears to brighten you might see that inside the cave there is a flurry of movement. Caution makes it sensible first to look around generally for larger forms of life before examining the roof and walls for its smaller forms. Sharks may sleep in caves, especially *Carcharias*, the nurse shark. This is a relatively harmless shark, with its small mollusc-eating mouth, but it is easily disturbed and, at up to 4 metres long, big enough to give a nasty bruise when it dashes in alarm towards the entrance. A large grouper at the back would cause no problem despite its size. There are several species and many common names of grouper but most are territorial and may occupy the same home for many years. In rare cases, some can reach a tremendously bulky length of 3 metres and these have a dangerous reputation in some parts of the world.

A moray, *Gymnothorax*, near the entrance also has a reputation of sorts, though possibly an overrated one. I remember being bitten by one when accidentally resting my hand on its head while collecting coral specimens. It was not a hard bite, more a gentle nip of warning that such intimacy was not welcomed. The blood had still looked green though, as it always does below a few metres deep. Morays like cave entrances. Their long tails are secure, while their heads protrude satisfactoriiy close to the bustle of activity near the entrance and outside. They seem entirely confident in their surroundings as they open and close their mouths rhythmically, pumping oxygenated water through their gills. Little cleaner shrimps may be observed in their mouths, foraging for scraps of flesh which are still attached to the moray's teeth. But once you are inside a cave it is discomforting to see a big moray near the entrance that was unnoticed as you entered. The performance of brushing past its nose must be repeated on the way out, this time knowing it is there.

(*Left*) The top lip of a cave entrance is often a rich area for attached colonies of animals. You can rarely tell until you pass inside whether the cave will be large or small, rich in life or relatively bare. But patterns of water currents usually mean that plenty of planktonic food swirls around the mouth.

(*Right*) The moray eel finds protective shelter in any size of cave or hollow in the rock. This spotted species is *Gymnothorax* and, like several other species, will avoid conflict with a diver unless severely provoked.

(*Left*) The solitary Coral trout, *Cephalopholis miniatus*, is territorial and may inhabit the same cave for many years. Some groupers can reach enormous sizes and should be paid the respect due to any large carnivorous fish, though most are retiring animals.

(*Right*) Looking out of a cave in a cliff face into open water presents a view with a natural frame of rock and sea fans. To most inhabitants of caves, there is no such thing as up or down; colonial animals hang down from the ceiling as readily as they grow up from the floor and fish also swim just as happily upside-down.

Another typical cave-dweller signals its presence more clearly with a flamboyant, fluttering display of large red fins as it sculls along a ledge. On the edges of the dorsal fin and the pair of pectorals are spines capable of injecting venom. This is *Pterois volitans*, the lion fish or dragon fish, and its colour is a warning. Unlike the highly venomous stone fish and scorpion fish that are encountered mostly on the shallow reef amongst rubble and which are both well camouflaged, the lion fish advertises both its presence and the fact that to touch it means severe pain and death to smaller creatures. Its consideration in this self-advertisement is to itself rather than to others, however. Potential predators have inherited instincts which tell them to leave this unmistakable fish alone.

Streaming in from the mouth of the cave may be enough light to make out the entire cavern, but a torch will highlight points of interest. The cave entrance itself is often the most spectacular sight from within; the mouth framed by rock and often curtained with sea fans, with hovering schools of tiny fish. Attached to the walls of the cave around the mouth will be encrusting red algae and representatives of the leafy or encrusting corals which contain zooxanthellae, but which are normally found only deep on the reef slopes. But, by the time the distance into the cave has increased to a metre or two, there is insufficient light to support even these and neither free-living nor symbiotic plants are found.

The fish inside a cave may be much more densely crowded than they are outside. Red, white or striped squirrel fish with huge eyes and golden damsel fish glint in the torchlight, swimming close to the walls and the roof as they do in probably every cave in the tropical seas. They hug the contours of the rock to such an extent that when they reach the roof of the cave they still hug it, belly towards the rock and upside-down. There they may remain or rest. Their response to the force of gravity is much less compelling than their response to the instinct which tells them to keep the rock beneath them. The small schools of upside-down fish are often the most conspicuous of the cave's inhabitants, but there are many more. Surveys have shown that over a hundred different species are sometimes present. Many of these are just chance and transient visitors, but

there are others that have opted for this environment, either for protection or because it is in here that they find their food.

There are plenty of shy, retiring animals of other groups as well. A discarded empty skeleton of a crayfish lying on the sand gives away the presence of one of the more spectacular of the resident crustaceans. This is not the remains of a dead animal, but the outworn armour of a living one and two large, twitching feelers projecting from a crevice above the skeleton show where it is. Like all crustaceans, its skeleton cannot grow as its body does and so it periodically casts it off to grow a new larger one. For a while, the animal is unprotected and even its claws are soft. At this time it is vulnerable and must seek shelter in a crevice. In another place, a kitchen midden of shells and crustacean skeletons (though this time skeletons which were certainly not discarded voluntarily) shows the presence of another shy predator—the octopus. Very common on some coral reefs and rare on others, these shell-less molluscs haul their catches back to their dens to feed, discarding the hard parts near their entrance, sometimes in untidy piles, but sometimes apparently building up a barrier between themselves and the outside world.

It is often the attached forms of life, however, which dominate the scene and give it much of its colour. The life attached to the walls and roof of a cave forms a microcosm of a lot of animals that are otherwise usually found in any number only much deeper on the reef. Some non-symbiotic corals are always present, especially the universal orange clumps of *Tubastraea* with their yellow tentacles. They may cover the roof completely in some caves. Occasional cup corals, *Caryophyllia* and *Desmophyllum*, with solitary polyps, will be scattered around, hoping their extended tentacles will come into contact with zooplankton, while a colonial close relative, *Polycyathus*, forms low, encrusting clumps when there is space. Green, flexible sea whips reach a metre or two out from the side walls, their stinging cells charged and ready to shoot at anything that triggers them with a touch, and several forms of smaller sea fan will commonly be found, apart from the giants screening the entrance.

Possibly the commonest animals in the cave will be

the hydroids. These, like sea fans, are colonies of small coelenterate animals supported by a structure of their own manufacture—and a very successful mode of life this seems to be. The structure and the life cycles of the component animals differ; they are usually called zooids rather than polyps, but they too depend on catching plankton from the water. They may be even better at killing it in fact, as their stings are particularly strong. Their structures are delicate and generally relatively small. Many of the dozens of species look like clumps of feathers, each feather being one colony: a central tough stalk with two rows of tiny zooids projecting off it from the sides. Clumps of twig-like structures are different species of hydroids, with a fuzzy appearance caused by the myriad of tiny extended animals which line and form the branches. Many of these colonies of animals, sometimes erroneously called stinging seaweed, pos-

Cardinal fish, such as this *Apogon*, are commonly seen in caves. This is partly because many of them are nocturnal and during the day retire into caves where they find protection.

sess stinging cells which are strong enough to leave a painful weal across the back of your hand or leg. They are closely related, in fact, to that equally painful hydrozoan called fire coral, or *Millepora*. They resemble each other in the structure of their zooids, even though without a microscope the large, stony-skeletoned fire coral looks more like other corals than a hydroid. Both have powerful stings in common, however, which are the most potent stings found amongst the attached coelenterate animals.

Between these projecting animal colonies are encrusting sponges, mainly reddish or brown in colour, occupying much of the wall that is not colonised by the coelenterates. They are a lowly form of animal

(*Left*) Fish continually stream in and out of a cave mouth, some passing in temporarily, others living in the cave and leaving occasionally on feeding trips. As many as one hundred different fish species have been found in a single cave.

(*Below*) Discarded remains of a crab's exoskeleton suggest that the crab has either moulted or fallen prey to an animal such as an octopus. In this case, remains of several different species suggests that they were eaten.

(*Left*) On a ledge in a cave, painted or spiny lobsters may be found. They detect movement and chemicals in the water with their sensitive feelers but, despite their armoured bodies, they are very retiring animals.

(*Right*) Hydroids are one of the commonest forms of cave-dwelling colonial animal. Each branch of the 'feathers' is one animal among the colonies of thousands. Some species sting fairly severely, but do not harm the brittle stars, which in this case are living in close commensal relationship with the hydroid.

life which also relies on plankton in the water. They pump large quantities of water through a series of filters of decreasing pore size within their bodies, straining out the particles of food. These animals are amongst the simplest forms of multicellular life, despite their often considerable size. They form an evolutionary side branch off the mainstream of animal life development, but their line has been around for over half a billion years. This pre-dates most other animals that we see by quite a long time so it is clear that they are a most successful group, despite their primitive bodies. Their cells do show a degree of differentiation, i.e. they have specialised jobs, with some creating the water current through the body, others trapping food and others working towards reproduction. But this must be a loose kind of specialisation, since you can break up a sponge, pass it through a sieve, and it will reform into one or many new sponges. Sponges have bodies made with several different minerals, but the majority of sponge bodies are mostly cavities and chambers whose arrangement and function allows large volumes of water to be pumped through them, so that the floating food can be extracted.

Large sponges harbour several smaller animals, such as crustaceans and fish, which obtain shelter in the cavernous chambers, and some have symbiotic bacteria in their tissues as well. They are not pre-dated on very much because most of their bulk is made up of inorganic minerals with no food value, but, as always, some animals, such as cowries, some nudibranchs and fish, such as the puffer fish, do feed on them.

Most of the biology of the cave-living animals, it seems, revolves around living on plankton or on dead particles suspended in the water. After all, what other forms of feeding are possible for animals which are fixed to rock in darkness for all their adult lives? The mobile animals have a greater choice, but the attached forms, which are often the most common, depend on microscopic, floating food.

Where does it all come from? Caves which have an abundance of life require large quantities of such food, which means a good exchange of water. But other caves can be remarkably barren. It all depends on water circulation. If there is relatively little ex-change of water then there will not be a rapidly renewed source of plankton passing through the cave. In that case, there can only be a small number of suspension-feeding animals. If there is a good exchange of water though, then the attached life responds accordingly. A large cavern with only one small aperture is a cul-de-sac and retains the same body of water within it for a long time. The amount of plankton in it would not be able to support much life for very long. But if the cave has other fissures, two openings possibly, or even an interlocking series of passages with other caves, then a through flow is assured, with the plankton being continually replenished. In this case, the life will be richer and more varied. The water flowing through a series of caverns gradually loses its load of particles as it goes. Although beginning relatively rich in plankton, it becomes strained of all it contains by the animal colonies en route, so that, when the water finally emerges again onto the surface of the reef, it is filtered water. The final parts of such a cave system may scarcely be able to support any life at all.

In a large cave, faint patches or shafts of light may be visible, showing where small apertures lead to the open reef but, even if there are no other openings through to the outside which are large enough to see, it is probable that water can still pass through. When you are next in a cave, look upwards and see your exhaled air collect on the ceiling, glinting like quicksilver and forming rivulets and shimmering pools. It does not stay very long, but trickles upwards through hundreds of tiny fissures. Viewed from the outside above the caves you would see countless streams of tiny bubbles coming out of the apparently solid rock itself and, for some while after the divers have left, these continue to rise as the trapped air slowly works its way upwards through the porous reef. In reefs in sheltered, sedimented waters in particular, where coral growth may not be at its best, the reef can be riddled with these fissures. Where the air can visibly pass through, then so can water, taking with it the suspended particles of food to the life inside.

Cave Formation

How are caves formed in reefs and then maintained

once they exist? There may be several ways, but three quite different processes together probably account for most.

A clue to the origins of one sort comes from the fact that a string of them may all be found at the same depth. Furthermore, they will be broad but not very deep or high. Very similar caves can be found at the present water level in other areas, excavated by the eroding action of centuries of waves. Now imagine what could have happened at an earlier time when the sea level was stationary for many centuries, but was at a lower level relative to the reef than it is today. This actually happened during the last Ice Ages of about 8000 years ago. It is reasonable to assume that, at that time, the waves eroded a line of cavities where they smashed against a wall of rock, just as they do today. And, just as it does today, suspended sand would have helped in the scraping process, acting like a liquid sandpaper. Then, when the sea level rose, the caves were drowned. Their size would depend partly on the exposure that the area suffered and for how long the process of erosion continued but once they were drowned by the rising sea they would be colonised by marine life again. Lines of caves, now sometimes little more than notches, may be seen at several depths, depending on the history of the area, but usually at not more than about 50 metres deep and commonly very much shallower.

The second way in which caves were formed would also have happened when the sea level was lower and the old reef blocks were high above the water. This time aerial erosion of the emerged rocky platforms was responsible. Acid rain can etch through limestone with comparative ease, so that during the centuries when rain fell on this rock irregular solution took place. Puddles excavated troughs and rivulets widened cracks with each succeeding year, etching out some of the largest and most complicated series of passages and caverns. Proof that rain can achieve prodigious feats of excavation can be seen in many old, fossil reefs that are now raised well above the sea. High vaulted caverns and tunnels thread their way through limestone hills in every continent on Earth. Along the floors of many flows a torrent which erodes the cavern making it ever larger, at least until the water finds or forces a lower route,

leaving the cavern dry. Along the walls and ceilings amongst the stalactites are patterns in the rock— fossil corals and other long dead creatures proving that this excavated cavern was once a reef below the sea.

Many of the more spectacular caves, such as the famous Blue Holes in the Caribbean, probably developed in this way, but so too did a greater number of smaller caves which are only a little less dramatic. But when the sea level rose again, when the ice caps melted, these were drowned and the erosion from these sources ceased.

The third way in which caves are formed differs from the previous ways as it is one which only happens underwater. Caves can be formed by the boring activities of animals and, as such, this process can happen independently of the other types of caves or it can continue to enlarge those caves formed above water after they have been drowned. The process happens mostly on reefs in sheltered waters which have reached their uppermost limits of growth at the low-tide level. The tops have then grown outwards and a steep side has resulted. The steep slopes and often turbid water which surrounds them are not the best environment for strong coral growth and, where such growth is poor, boring exceeds the deposition of new rock. Each tunnel made by a boring sponge or mollusc is very small but, when millions of them all attack a section of the wall, their combined assault may result in serious weakening of the structure. Collapse may occur and, over the centuries, caves will slowly form in the back reef conditions.

But however a cave is formed, its maintenance is a complicated thing. Almost at once, the growth of life in many of them, though often small, is enough to start the volume shrinking. An even bigger cause of infill comes from sand pumped in by water movements. Both factors may continue until the cavern is filled up again. Where the current is just right, however, sand may not be deposited in the cave so that it remains unfilled and accessible as a home to thousands of cryptic species. It is a dynamic and changing process, just like all the other factors which make and shape the reef. Today's caverns may not exist tomorrow, while tomorrow's caves may still be solid rock today.

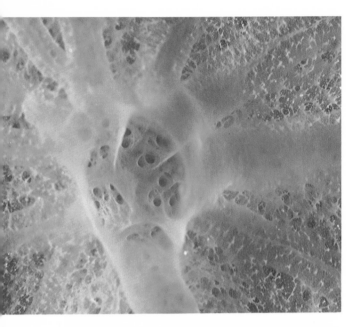

Three quite different and unrelated forms of cave-dwelling animal which all feed in very similar ways are shown. The sponges (*left*) in caves are usually flat encrusting sheets, whose main bulk is taken up by a series of chambers and passages. Water is pumped through these and food particles are extracted. This shows the exhalant openings of a large one. The delicate soft coral, *Dendronephthya* (*right*), hanging from the roof of a cave, catches passing plankton with its stinging cells. The clam, *Spondylus* (*below*), is one of the largest of the non-colonial animals which cement themselves to cave walls. It too feeds on plankton which it filters from water pumped through its body. Sometimes the shells of groups of these add large amounts of limestone to the walls of the caves. Other organisms live on the shells, concealing them well.

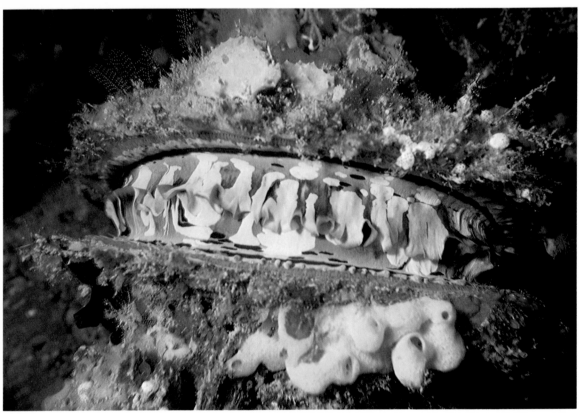

(*Below*) Tomorrow's caves. One of the main ways in which caves can develop is by the formation of notches at sea level. If the sea level rises in the future, as it has done before, these notches will be drowned to form characteristic long but narrow caves.

10. WORLD OF TWILIGHT

BENEATH the coral gardens the water becomes still. The wave surge goes completely and is replaced only by a gentle sideways drift. As you descend along the reef slope you might pass through a *thermocline*—a sudden transition in temperature which indicates the line where two bodies of water meet. The lower one is several degrees colder and the transition may be so clearly defined that you can have one hand in the upper body of warm water and the other in the colder bottom layer. Many reefs here plunge fairly steeply and it begins to darken because of the increasing mass of water through which the light has to pass. A strange thing happens to the light which does pass through; it changes in quality and becomes a misty blue. Even where the water is so clear that a diver can look up and see the surface 50 metres above him, everything is a shade of blue—even the powerful disk of the sun. The reef and all it contains is seen in monochrome, and it is no longer colourful.

A Shade of Blue

The light deep on the reef is blue because water is a selective filter of light. Sunlight is made up of every colour in the rainbow and, when it passes through water, each colour behaves differently. Red is absorbed from the sun's spectrum after a very few metres; orange and yellow after just a little more. Blue light alone passes through to great depths and, at the foot of the reef, it adds a dreamlike, ethereal

quality to the scene. Black objects, such as some tall branching corals, stay black, but so too do many others which are really a multiplicity of colour. Things which are red or yellow at the surface look that way because they reflect back at the observer the red or yellow components of the sunlight. But when no red or yellow exists it obviously cannot be reflected. So the object can only look black, or possibly blue if it can reflect a little of that. However, a diver need do one thing only to bring everything to colour and that is turn on a torch. Its white light reintroduces all the colours of the spectrum so that every object which the beam touches is painted with colour. Sponges, the encrusting red algae and even the red spots on a grouper stand out because of the reflected red light, at least until the torch moves on. If a photographer is there, sudden pulses of light from the camera flash illuminate a wider area and the deeper and dimmer it is, the stronger is the effect of a sudden flood of colour. This is why colour photography here needs artificial light, not only because of the low light level but because addition of the white light turns the blue monochrome into colour.

The change of quality and the fall in intensity of the light deep on the reef has a great importance to the life there. Plants, and this includes of course the symbiotic algae in the corals, need light and many plants need particular colours or wavelengths of it. If the necessary colours are not available—and in deep water they may not be—then special pigments are required to aid the working of the chlorophyll. Plants which do not have these special pigments cannot exist. Therefore, species of plants which can tolerate low levels of blue light begin to replace the shallow forms. Even on a reef which has very clear water, this becomes obvious as the 30-metre mark is reached.

It affects the corals too. All the large brain and branching corals are left behind in the sunlit regions above and other species take their place. Most of these are leafy and fragile, foliaceous forms mixed with small encrusting species. There is no wave action down here, even in the severest storms, so physically-strong skeletons are much less important to the corals. Here the leaves are so fragile that they can even break under their own weight, which, buoyed in water as they are, seems minimal. Down here a clumsy diver or a boat's anchor can cause havoc.

At 40 metres, several corals with a leafy form are evident. A common one is the tramline coral, *Pachyseris*, distinctive because of the parallel ridges and grooves which run concentrically round its surface. There are the plates of *Echinopora* and *Mycedium*, and particularly delicate ones which belong to the genus *Leptoseris*. All are attached by a small part of their underside only, while the plate expands outwards from the reef. The plates of these deep species rarely thicken as all spare energy is channelled into expanding their surface area.

One partly unsolved puzzle lies here. It is known that it is the same species of algae which lives in both deep and shallow corals. It grows and multiplies in corals at 100 metres deep at light levels which are only one-thousandth of that in shallow water, so this plant is capable of considerable adaptation. But it is thought to be partly the light requirement which determines which corals live at which depths on the reef. The differences must lie in the animal part of the symbiotic relationship. The processes of budding and reproducing, metabolising and depositing a skeleton all require energy. Deep down there is less light energy available and so smaller, thinner skeletons are usual. Some experiments have shown that leafy corals can grow well in shallower conditions if they are artifically placed there and protected from damaging waves but, as they do not live there naturally, they clearly lack the competitive edge for

shallow-water living. They do have the edge, however, for deep-water living, and in the depths, where competition is less, they thrive.

A second group of corals becomes more conspicuous at the foot of the reef. These are the forms which lack symbiotic algae. They grow more slowly than the symbiotic species and are apparently less competitive still so that they are relatively rare in well-lit areas. But deeper down, where the symbiotic species thin out, those lacking the algae appear in greater numbers. Light is of no direct consequence to them and they depend for food entirely on what they can catch with their tentacles. Large species of one sort, *Dendrophyllia*, may dominate the reef with their large black bushy skeletons over a metre tall. Where they are common, they can be locally significant in the process of reef building and a closer look at the coral rubble of the area will show that a lot of it is derived from this species. But most of the corals of this group which are found on the reef are small and generally of minor consequence.

Although species lacking symbiotic algae cannot tolerate the heavy competition in the coral gardens, they come into their own at the bottom of the reef and beyond. The ones we see on the reef are only the uppermost-reaching representatives of a vast and complex group that lies far deeper than our range. Their various members can live on submarine mountain ranges and in the abyssal depths, and extend to Polar regions. Without plant cells to limit their range, they have radiated out to every marine habitat in every ocean. They may not form reefs as we mean it, but they can live in thick banks at great depth. At over 100 metres deep in the Caribbean, the colonial coral, *Oculina*, forms extensive banks, while far to the north in the cold Atlantic the related *Lophelia* does the same. Both of these corals are branching, with thin arms to support their polyps above the thick sediment that covers much of their adopted habitat.

Altogether there are about as many species of very deep-water coral as there are species which build reefs, but most are rarely seen. Many of them are not restricted, in the way that their symbiotic relatives are, to one or other of those two great coral provinces, the Atlantic and the Indo-Pacific. Instead, because they are not confined to warm waters, they

(*Left*) As you descend the reef, the seascape changes; familiar species disappear and are replaced by others. Only blue light filters down this far. The foreground on the reef is illuminated by the camera flash and shows that red is in fact a dominant colour amongst deep-water organisms. But under natural light alone, everything appears in shades of blue, as seen on the more distant part of the reef which lies beyond the range of the flash.

(*Right*) A cascade of leafy coral called *Pachyseris* marks a point on many Indo-Pacific reefs where the deep reef can be said to begin. These colonies are very thin and delicate, although each colony here is about a metre across. In the Caribbean, the similarly shaped *Agaricia* is characteristic of deeper zones.

(*Left*) The steep reef slope is characteristic of many parts of the world. The monochromatic light makes the deep reef a tranquil but dramatic place to dive.

(*Right*) An extreme close-up of the above leafy coral, *Pachyseris*, shows the symmetry on the surface of this beautiful coral.

(*Far right*) The black branching coral, *Dendrophyllia*, comes into its own where light diminishes. This is representative of the group which does not contain symbiotic algae and so it is not restricted to well-lit areas.

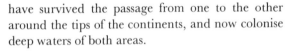

have survived the passage from one to the other around the tips of the continents, and now colonise deep waters of both areas.

Solid Foundations

Quite a lot of mystery surrounds the structure of the deepest part of the coral reef and a lot remains to be discovered about its role in the life and growth of the whole atoll or coral bank but, in whatever way the reef originally formed, this now deep area was once itself in shallow water where the light was strong. Then it was the site of flourishing and rapid coral growth and, at that time, it actively expanded outwards. Now it is deeply submerged and is a foundation for the present shallow reef.

To what extent the now deep reef is growing or being eroded is difficult to say. Here, as much as anywhere, destruction of the fabric of the reef is

Sea fans, or gorgonians, generally steal the scene in deep water. Three photographs of similar species show increasingly enlarged views: the entire colony (*left*), 2 metres tall and wide, showing the veined supporting structure; a section of a multi-coloured fan (*top*); and a close-up of the edge of a colony (*above*). In the last, the natural width of the section is only 10 centimetres and oblique lighting shows up the rows of tiny, expanded polyps along the top and under-surface of each arm. The polyps capture passing plankton. The entire fan is always orientated across the current (i.e. in all the pictures the current flows into the page) so that these colonies present a very large food-capturing area.

going on. Erosion by biological forces is considerable and probably not less than that in the coral gardens above. As before, sponges bore deeply by secreting acid and the limestone provides an easy medium for the tunnelling activities of burrowing bivalves. So erosion proceeds apace.

On the construction side, there seems at first sight to be several problems. The first is the relatively poor

coral growth. As we have seen, growth becomes increasingly slow compared with its rapid pace above and is likely to provide only a small plus in the construction ledger below about 40 metres. It does add something though. Other groups help to make up the difference and an important one is that of calcareous red algae. These cover a greater proportion of the hard substrate than the corals do over a depth range of perhaps 40 metres, until they too die out. These red algae are strong reef builders. In the shallowest, surf beaten areas, it will be remembered, there are scarcely any corals at all and yet that area bears the main force of the sea's weathering. We saw that the reason why that region survived and grew was due to red algae. In a similar way other members of this group of plants become increasingly important on the deep reef, so that here too they add more to the total reef material than do the corals.

More assistance in the building process comes

On the Caribbean reefs, gorgonians are often more common than on Indo-Pacific reefs. Many are less branched and have a more three-dimensional structure than the typical fan of the Indo-Pacific.

from a fairly unexpected source: the sponges. Most are fairly slow-growing animals and, although their bodies contain stony lattices or spicules, most are rather fragile and leave little of substance behind when they die. Their main contribution does not usually come from limestone deposition. Until recently sponges were considered to be neutral at best in the reef-building process—and their boring members of course are very destructive. Recent research in the Caribbean, however, shows that they can provide a great binding capacity in which they hold coral fragments together for long enough to allow other agencies to cement them. This happens to some extent without the sponges, but they appear to help considerably. Furthermore, other sponges,

Sponges occupy a greater proportion of the reef surface in deep water. The stony spicules of sponges like this add a little to the sand when they die, but the bulk of their bodies disintegrates. Unlike corals, they are not reef builders.

Some sponges which spread between corals and rock may assist in reef building a little by binding loose material together for a while but, at these depths, reef building has probably largely ceased. These animals feed on the gentle rain of debris that falls from the shallows and on plankton.

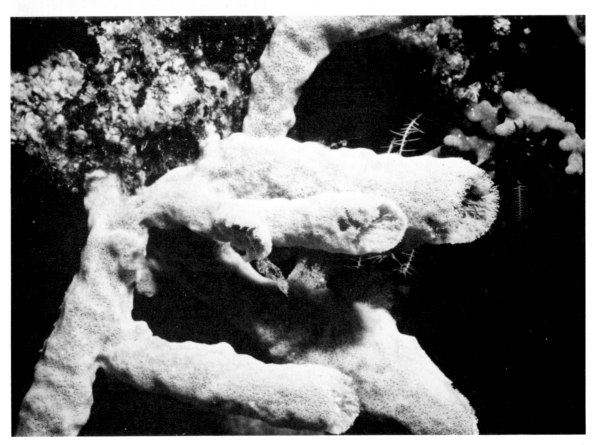

themselves made of a hard stony material, have recently been found in caves and deep areas of the reef. These are the *sclerosponges* and they behave in a way similar to corals, directly depositing substantial amounts of limestone which, by one estimate, is several times stronger than concrete.

Probably the main source of reef material in the depths is that which grew in shallow water. Tonnes of sand from ground-up corals stream down the slope to come to rest where the waves themselves can no longer disturb it. Some of the enormous quantities that find their way here fill the holes and are overgrown by algae to become cemented, ending up as part of the matrix of the reef. The strong waves and bioerosion, which are so destructive to living corals in the shallows and which result in so much sand production, are now seen to be responsible for the continual addition of reef-building materials further down. In fact, the destructive processes of the shallows are, if anything, an ally in the constructive processes deep on the reef.

This may work for slopes where the flow of sand can be arrested in crevices and on less steep slopes, but not much sand will come to rest on vertical expanses. On these there is little actual growth. Less light falls upon a vertical face than on a horizontal one, so only a few outward-reaching corals and those without symbiotic algal cells can grow. Sometimes only small sponges, some algae and large cemented molluscs join these corals in keeping a hold. This leads to some spectacular sights, because, regardless of the lack of growth or even net erosion of the cliff, the shallow coral gardens above it keep on growing. These grow upwards and outwards to overhang the vertical cliff beneath to an alarming degree. Then the inevitable happens—the foundation gives way and the section of reef slumps. An enormous mass of overhanging coral crashes down in an avalanche of rock, gouging a pale scar in the side of the reef. Depending on the slope below, it may come to rest within diving range to provide a spectacular, broken terrain, or it may plough on to unknown depths. On a small scale it happens often.

A diver would be lucky—or perhaps unlucky—to witness one of these slumps happening, but it is common on some cliffs to see the pale, bare scars which are clear indications of recent slumps. Each may be one or several metres across and extend downwards for perhaps 100 metres, big enough to make a lasting impression on the reef. Giant slumps are more rare but they do occur; they have been known to cause the loss of entire, cultivated islands which lay on the rim of an atoll with steep sides. The scars of landslides will eventually fade as they are colonised by opportunistic species, until the top again grows out too far.

Below the 60-metre mark, the scene may change again. The surface is now near the limit of even the best visibility and only twilight blue filters down. The many reefs which sit on continental shelves may terminate now, flattening out to a near-horizontal plain covered by sand and silt. Oceanic atolls, however, and other reefs which arise from much deeper water, have seaward reefs which continue down, perhaps with the occasional sandy terrace, but essentially with a steep slope to way beyond our vision. Compared to the brighter regions above, life seems more scarce, but there is still plenty around. The surface of the rock still has a cover of sponges and algae which show up red in a torch beam, while sea fans and sea whips project outwards for several metres.

Different species of fish and larger versions of many others are more common here: hump-headed wrasse of enormous dimensions, a grouper of over 450 kilograms and the tail-less sunfish with big floppy fins, saucer-shaped and standing 2 metres tall. A few solitary sharks, including oceanic species, may also show an interest. Where a narrow plain of highly-reflective sand has accumulated the scene is lightened and vision may be clear for 40 metres in all directions. A patchy forest of a new form of life may be seen for the first time; bushes of fine grey-black twigs which, like the sea fans, are attached to the rock. This is precious black coral, called *Antipatharia*, whose branches can be cleaned and polished to provide a glossy ebony-black material that has a market in the jewellery trade. It is not a true coral, despite its name; nor is it closely related to the sea fans which it more closely resembles. Like them both, however, it is a coelenterate, a colonial animal whose countless tiny polyps collectively deposit a skeletal structure in typical manner. Their occurrence is sporadic and

One of the precious black corals, *Antipathes*, from the Atlantic. Like a hydroid in appearance but forming bigger bushes, this has a flexible skeleton which can take a high polish and is made into beads and other forms of jewellery.

probably non-existent on reefs where collectors have visited but, on occasion, rich expanses can be found in relatively shallow water if the conditions are just right for it. It is becoming an endangered organism.

Occasionally interspersed amongst the sparse forests of colonial coelenterates, in this twilight world of matt blues and greys, there may be some highly luminescent coral colonies. They shine out in a vivid orange which catches your attention from a long way off. These are a form of branched coral called *Madracis*, although other corals can behave like this too. They contain a pigment which absorbs the ambient blue light and then re-emits a strong orange glow, whose contrast is as startling as a beacon at this depth.

Further down, the changes continue slowly. Below 60 metres, no detailed studies by divers operating with the usual SCUBA apparatus can be done, but there have been surveys from submersibles. These have shown that, in both the Caribbean and the Indo-Pacific, algae and leafy symbiotic corals can extend in some cases to nearly 100 metres deep, becoming sparser all the time. Below this point, only sponges and those corals and other coelenterates which do not need light may grow. This is the base of the coral reef as we know it. Most of it now is covered with sand or silt, but even where there is rocky substrate covered with life, it is no longer recognisable as a coral reef.

Limits to Deep Diving

Unfortunately for those who wish to explore the deeper parts of the reef, several factors reduce the safety and the time which can be spent at depth. This has also reduced the amount that we have discovered about this area. For every increase in depth of 10 metres, the water pressure rises by 1 atmosphere so that at 50 metres, for example, the body is subjected to an additional pressure of 5 atmospheres, caused by the column of water above. It goes unnoticed in one sense, but not by the body tissues. The inhaled air taken in from the cylinders on the diver's back surges into the bloodstream and from there into all the body tissues. The rate at which this happens increases with the pressure, but it does not happen in a straightforward way. Instead, its absorption accelerates with each increment of depth and the blood and tissues fill up with dissolved gases. When the diver surfaces the pressure is reduced, so the gases—mainly nitrogen— surge out again. If the deep diver surfaces slowly this happens in a controlled way and there is no problem. But if he surfaces too quickly bubbles may form in the body causing great pain—the *bends*—with severe and permanent effects. So surfacing must be done slowly. After particularly deep or long dives, this is supplemented in practice by stopping at certain depths for certain lengths of time. This process can easily take longer than the entire working part of the dive, so commonly such lengthy practices are sensibly avoided by limiting the depth or duration of the dive to make such stops unnecessary. But, if a deep dive is undertaken, these stops must be made and their calculation is one of the most important safety considerations of all.

A second effect gives problems at these depths. This is again caused by that supposedly inert gas, nitrogen. Its effect on the brain when under pressure is that of a narcotic and can be severe. Disorientation, blurriness and loss of faculties, including memory, are symptoms. Exhilaration often accompanies it too, giving this narcosis the common name of *rapture of the deep*, or it may be experienced as depression. It may come upon a diver slowly or suddenly and may differ in severity on different days. It may also be experienced at shallower depths than 20 or 30 metres in some cases.

A third most dangerous effect occurs deeper still,

40 metres deep and surfacing towards the light.

caused this time by oxygen. Although this is the essential, life-sustaining part of the atmosphere, when breathed in under a pressure of 8 atmospheres or more, air is highly toxic, causing extreme nervous activity, including loss of consciousness, which at these depths is invariably fatal. A SCUBA diver should never approach such depths. Mechanisms do exist for diving at these depths and far beyond, but these involve the use of special apparatus and artificial breathing mixtures in which the concentrations of oxygen and nitrogen are much reduced and replaced by relatively harmless ones such as helium.

These features make it difficult and impractical to undertake very much in the deeper areas of the coral reef. Probably they will be overcome one day, but in any case, it is in the relatively shallow areas where sunlight penetrates that life is at its richest, and in many senses the coral reef can be said to end when light becomes too dim for plants to grow and for corals to deposit the limestone which is the foundation of the reef.

11. ISLANDS OF CORAL

ERCHED atop those living, dying, growing, eroding, changing and evolving rocky structures sit the tiniest scraps of land. Barely higher than the high-tide level, coral islands maintain a precarious existence just a few steps ahead of forces which would level them down. Some are transient features which cannot survive a storm but which appear again year after year, while others have a crown of vegetation and, in terms of a few years or centuries anyway, are here to stay. These islets are the caps of sub-sea hills and even mile-high mountains which, in the manner of an iceberg, are mostly underwater.

How do such islands form on the top of a reef above the sea when the reef itself can only grow up to the low-tide level? Two ways at least are possible.

(*Above*) Some coral islands are mere blocks of limestone protruding above the water. These are old reefs which probably formed when the sea level was higher than it is now in relation to the reef. This block is now exposed above sea level. It is constantly eroded by waves and rain and may one day be worn back to sea level.

(*Left*) Many coral islands are formed when particular patterns of waves and currents pile sand and rubble up into banks. A block of rock, such as that in the previous photograph, may also help by providing a stable core for the sand to pile up against. These terns quickly colonise islands, laying their eggs on the sand amongst the rubble. Plants soon follow but, for a long time, may not be able to last for longer than the food reserves in their seeds and nuts allow.

Some coral islands rise up from the sea to a few metres in minature cliffs. These are solid limestone and embedded in them you may find the remains of long dead coral colonies. In such cases, you are looking at a raised reef, something which clearly grew below the level of the water, whatever its present level may be. In some cases, this would be caused by an uplift of the sea bed below the reef, pushing it upwards above the water level. In other cases, it is the result of past sea-level changes caused by the global climate and the Ice Ages. When, in millenia long past, the sea was higher than it is today relative to the land, reefs built upwards to that level. Later the water fell to far below its present position, leaving the newly-made reefs high and dry. Erosion wore them down a great deal in succeeding centuries and the sea rose up again, but not enough to cover them completely. The result in both cases is the same and has resulted in islands of old coral reef.

The second type of island arises when coral debris accumulates on top of a living reef, piling up because of the patterns of currents and waves. These islands are at first quite unsuitable for life. Many shift each season and even disappear completely on occasions. But some become stable. When they do, plants begin to colonise them. The initial vegetation may be grasses and low bushy plants which can survive in salty sand, for that is all the islands are at this stage. These help to bind the shifting sand and slowly top-soil increases. Birds which have visited the island from the start add nutrients in their droppings and

The end result. A beach of coral sand upon a coral island in a coral sea.

Near the end of a rainy week in an abandoned coconut plantation. The path is a stream and the ground beneath it a swamp, but it sustains the water table and keeps the salt water at bay and is the reason for the prolific plant growth. Heavy downpours can leach away nutrients, however, so a little rain and often is the best way for the plants. Without rain, this area reverts to a baked crust after just a few weeks.

more and bigger plants appear. The occasional coconut may self-seed too. As plants become more diverse and bigger, so do the birds, each generating favourable conditions for the other. The island becomes still more secure and stable.

These islands are also known as *low islands* because of their height. This distinguishes them from *high islands*, which are made from granite or volcanic rock and which have a quite different character, even though they may be fringed by coral reefs. Low islands are the true coral islands, made only of the softer limestone.

Given favourable circumstances, coral islands come to be idyllic places, small crowded communities which fittingly cap the reefs on which they stand. One of the requirements for this development is the presence of fresh water.

Rain

Beaches of coral islands do not always look like a stage set for an advertisement for rum. Days do exist when all is not sparkling sand, mirror calm seas and gently rustling palm leaves. Days exist, in fact, when scudding cloud forms ten-tenths cover, when the wind bends the palm trees 30 degrees over, up to and beyond their breaking point, pulling off the heavy fronds and coconuts. The seas breaking on the edges of the reef become mountainous, the waves reaching 10 metres high, which is sobering on low islands whose highest point is only 3 metres above sea level. But it is the rain which makes it more memorable yet.

When the annual monsoon trough, a nearby cyclone or just a rainy squall hits the island, precipitation can reach 30 cm in a day for several days on end. It may be difficult to understand this when the rain seems to be driving horizontally. Driven in sheets that swamp you and rods that sting you, it comes with such force that the rain gauge is knocked over anyway. Well-laced with salty foam, it penetrates every pore and you feel wetter than you do when diving and thoroughly cold, even on the Equator. The paths which wind across the coconut or banana groves become lakes of mud, squelching through your toes as you run back to the shelter of a house or tent, hoping to close the shutters or tent flaps before everything is a soggy mess.

Heavy rain may last for several months in certain places and seasons; in others, the squall may end as suddenly as it started after just a few hours. In all cases, much fresh water floods off the land onto the reef flats, the rest penetrating the soil and porous rock of the island. This part forms a freshwater lens beneath the surface of the island, slightly above the level of the sea. It is a life-giving water table which keeps the salt away and the vegetation of the island depends on it. While rain is plentiful, life will thrive.

It is when the rain does not come and the strong sun is shining that conditions for life become difficult on the island. It may be cool and damp enough for ferns beneath the canopy of green, but at the top of the canopy and at the edges of the trees or shrubs by the water's edge, the heat may be fierce, baking the sand or rock nearly to the temperature of boiling water. The sun on the vegetation induces tremendous water loss as plants transpire to keep themselves cool. This water must be replaced continually via the roots from the fresh-water table. If the water table fails, so do the plants and animals which depend on it. On coral cays or on the tiny islands of a coral atoll where topsoil is thin and no part of the land is more than a couple of hundred metres from the shore, the rain must also be frequent to prevent the sea water from seeping inwards.

Beach Life

At the shoreline live only a few specially adapted plants. It is an area periodically soaked by salt water, and has a soil which is sometimes nothing but sand. Fewer animals and plants live here.

One group of animals in particular, however, has occupied this area more than any other. This is the domain of the crabs and hermit crabs, many of which live mostly on the land while others are quite content on either side of the water's edge.

Life here, especially for the larger crabs, is one of scavenging. The action of the waves, reduced now by the expanse of reef flat to a relatively gentle force, constantly brings organic debris. This is dumped on the water's edge, mostly at the high tide mark or strand line. There is plenty of nutrition left in this debris and crabs especially make good use of it. Added to the debris of marine origin, there is a lot of terrestrial plant material from strand-line shrubs and trees, all of which may add up to a substantial bulk of food.

The numerous crabs compete with each other for this food. Some race quickly about, even in the heat of the noonday sun, while others are nocturnal. Tunnels 10 centimetres wide in a sandy beach are the home of the ghost crab, *Ocypode*, which shelters during the heat in its cooler moist burrow, emerging to feed at night. Other crabs, with eyes on stalks, periodically dash into the sea especially when disturbed, leaving only their eyes above the water, ever watchful for shore birds. Tiny crustaceans, such as amphipods, collect in large numbers amongst the debris of the strand line; these too can burrow if disturbed. To live beneath the sand, or to be able to temporarily hide there, is a common adaptation for shore life, providing as it does a refuge from both heat and predation. Amongst their hunters are other carnivorous crustaceans and, especially, sea birds whose long sharp beaks easily penetrate a crab's shell.

The most conspicuous crab on many beaches is the

(*Above*) The burrowing crab, *Ocypode*, excavates a tunnel cease-lessly. If it digs below the high-tide level, it will have to do it again the next day. When these, and similar burrowing crabs, burrow further towards the interior of the island, they perform the same function as the earthworm: mixing the surface layers of leaf litter and sand.

(*Above right*) A lot of myth surrounds the coconut crab and its eating habits. It can and does eat coconuts, using its immensely powerful claws to tear them, but will also eat more easily-obtained fruit if it can. This medium-sized specimen makes good use of the fruit *Papaya*, in an abandoned pawpaw plantation.

Hermit crabs are one of the most conspicuous parts of coral-shore life. They scavenge almost anything, including broken twigs of shoreline-dwelling plants. Although they live on the shore, they lay eggs in the sea.

hermit crab. This type of crab has a soft and vulnerable abdomen and protects itself by backing into and hanging onto an empty mollusc shell. These heavily-laden animals are really remarkably agile, able to climb branches of shrubs and sprint fairly rapidly across the sand. Because the shells they inhabit have a right-handed coil, their abdomens have had to coil as well in order to fit into the shells. As a result, their abdominal appendages on the right have become much smaller or lost completely. On their abdomens, however, they possess structures which serve to anchor them to the inside of the shell. The shell no longer grows now that the original mollusc owner is dead and absent, so the hermit crab has to periodically replace its home with a larger one as its body grows. Usually shells are scattered about on the beach for the taking. Sometimes a major reshuffling of shells takes place amongst a group of hermits, and occasionally a fight may occur between two crabs, one pulling on another for hours until the

victim is killed or releases the shell. Very rarely one is seen without a shell, when it makes an easy meal for a tern.

Living as they do on the beach or strand-line, hermit crabs live in close association with the sea. One relative of it has moved to a life more independent of the sea than any other crustacean. This is the large coconut or robber crab. Called *Birgus latro*, this tree-climbing giant can reach half a metre long and has immensely powerful claws. As a young adult, it wears a shell like a hermit crab, but when it outgrows the largest shell, it carries about a half coconut instead. Eventually the slow-growing animal outgrows even this and abandons any protection, relying on its hardened exoskeleton and its claws. It has a close association with the coconut all through life, wearing it when small, lining its burrows with the husks and eating the nut itself. Quite an unsociable animal, it competes vigorously with other coconut crabs for food, when it is a matter of the biggest winning. They forage well inland, but they have not lost all association with the sea; the female must return to the sea to lay her eggs. The larvae then disperse in the sea, just like the larvae of all other crabs, until, as small adults, they crawl again up the beach into the shrubs and trees.

Of all the beach life, the turtles are the most majestic, although they are of course not resident; females come merely to lay eggs. They are normally seen under or on the surface of the water for most of the year, but they come ashore at the appropriate season and conditions of tide once a year, dragging their heavy bodies up the beach to the belt of shrubs just above the water line. Greens and hawksbills, the Ridley, loggerhead and leatherback, all leave the sea for a night.

The egg-laying and then the hatching after many weeks is synchronised by the moon and tides. Then, after the determined time has passed, the hatchlings emerge from their eggs and climb up to the surface of the sand. Unfortunately for the hatchlings, the sea birds know the timing too and devour many young turtles as they dash down to the water. In the sea, predatory fish eat many more so that only a few survive. This is the way of life for most marine species; many offspring are produced so that one or two

Majestic green turtles climb out of the sea onto the beaches, mostly at night, to dig a nest and lay eggs. This digging is a laborious process which takes the female a couple of hours. Even then she may not lay eggs in the hole if she is not satisfied with it and will return to the sea, presumably to try later.

When the shrubs, *Scaevola* and *Tournefourtia*, arrive to grow and stabilise the shore, the island has a better chance of surviving. Pink-footed boobies nest in them and add a lot of fertiliser, thus helping the plants. These birds are fish-eaters, so they cause a transfer of nutrient from the rich reef to the nutrient-starved island, thus boosting the cycle of growth.

survive for long enough to reach maturity themselves.

In a sense, the turtle and coconut crab are opposites. The crab lives on land and returns to the sea to spawn; the turtle lives in the sea and returns to land to lay eggs. This is simply because neither species has made a complete evolutionary transition to its chosen environment from that which its ancestors had. Ancestrally, the coconut crab was marine and the turtle was terrestrial. Each changed its habitat in a slow process, which is probably still continuing, but which has not reached completion. Both must still begin life in the environment of their heritage and not the surrounds of their adulthood. Hatching seems to be the most difficult process to change.

The plant life of the foreshore and beach is one of the most important defences that a low coral islet has against the eroding waves. Some creepers, such as *Ipomea*—the sea morning glory—or shrubs such as *Scaevola* and *Tournefortia* live at the high-tide mark and above. Here they are rooted in the sand. Where they grow, the sand is stabilised to a very large extent and is prevented from shifting in high seas or during daily high tides. These plants literally preserve the beaches and protect the coastal areas which otherwise would become washed away. As they increase in density, their leaf litter, together with droppings from birds nesting in their branches, add organic matter to the otherwise lifeless sand. Not much accumulates compared to further inland as every high spring tide flushes some away. But these foreshore plants have all that they require to sustain life in this area between land and coral reef.

Shorelines on the seaward side of atolls, and in other areas which are exposed to more severe waves than even these plants can cope with, show a lot of bare limestone rock. In the intertidal part there may be a few hardy molluscs, such as *Nerita* and *Planaxis*, which feed on the sparse patches of algae, but the diversity of life is very small. Above the intertidal region, there may be nothing visible living at all yet micro-organisms may grow in a film over some of the rock. Here, where occasional strong sea conditions scour the island just above the high-tide level back to bare rock, there is the least diversity of life found anywhere on coral reefs, or coral islands.

(*Top*) The fortunes of islands can change, even when they have become well colonised by vegetation. As the reef and weather changes, a small shift in the pattern of currents means that, instead of sand being added to the shore, it is here being stripped away. Palm trees have their roots undermined so they topple and this island tip is shrinking. Probably the process will soon stabilise again, with the island attaining a changed shape. Sand may be dumped at the other end so it may not shrink in overall size.

(*Above*) Solid rock inclining down towards the sea is characteristic of many coral-island shores. Its formation is still not quite understood but may result from the effect of micro-organisms and the actions caused at the interface of sea and fresh water. This durable material is significantly more resistant to wave erosion than sand. This area is usually the most hostile to life and supports only a very few, very hardy species.

Mangrove Areas

Along many of the coral seas, the fringe between the reef and island is colonised by a different group of plants. These are forests of mangrove trees. They are derived from many different tree families, but they share in common an ability to tolerate high levels of salt and low levels of oxygen around their roots. Mangroves develop mostly along the shores of continents between the land and offshore coral reefs, but they commonly colonise the offshore reefs themselves, forming thick forests even on oceanic atolls.

Unlike the stabilising shrubs found on the beaches, these plants grow at a level where their roots are continually or at least periodically immersed in salt water. Their roots can exclude a lot of the salt when they take up water, but many supplement their salt-resisting process by excreting it from their leaves as well. Eventually, on a reef flat which has a suitable substrate, and especially in shallows where there is a lot of muddy runoff from the land, these trees form a thick forest. They stabilise the substrate and trap more silt, perpetuating their own preferred environment. But this increasingly muddy environment lacks oxygen. The roots of even these trees need oxygen and so they have developed *knee roots* or *aerial roots*, which have parts protruding above the surface into the air. These breathe and transport oxygen into the immersed sections. At ground level, the mass of roots and trunks forms an almost impenetrable forest, which gives stability to the shore line and otherwise shifting substrate, which is most important in protecting the coasts from erosion.

Just as the trees themselves form a discrete and unique forest of plants at the water's edge, so there is a unique community of animals living amongst them. Many molluscs and crustaceans especially inhabit the base of the forest. Several species of oysters live on the roots, the only firm substrate to which they can attach themselves. Gastropods may also crawl on the roots, careful not to fall into the anoxic mud in which they would perish. It is here too that

(*Left*) Mangrove trees often colonise reef flats around coral islands, as on Low Isles on the Great Barrier Reef. Behind the camera was a thick forest of the plants, covering several acres. This scene is of the outmost edge of that forest and shows the coral reef and deeper water beyond. Long arching roots, coming from well above the water, curve down to provide support for the trees.

(*Above*) A skyline of coconut palms signals man's past activities on many coral islands. Economics change and most remote copra plantations are no longer used, but the changes caused to the island ecosystems are longer-lasting.

some of the most remarkable fish of all are found in great numbers; mudskippers which can climb out of the water and into the roots themselves and, where the water is brackish, archer fish which can fell a flying insect with a well-directed jet of water.

Many forms of life which are dependent for their food on the leaves dropped by the mangrove trees are found in the adjacent waters. A still closer link between these forests and the reefs offshore is made by several larger fish and crustaceans which move between the two environments. For many, such as the lobster, the mangroves provide a nursery for hatching young, which, when larger, move off to the coral reef. These forests, which may form just a thin ribbon between the land and the reef, are biologically as well as physically linked to the coral reef.

Further inland

The large, unspoiled coral island which exists in a natural state is unfortunately becoming more and more difficult to find. Small islets which are untouched by man's activities are more common, but those large enough to have provided a home for man have usually been severely disturbed. Even islands around the rims of the most remote atolls have been inhabited, even if only for short and interupted periods. Further inland on a coral island, therefore, we see a biological community which has changed to varying degrees.

On many, there is evidence that considerable forests of hardwood trees once flourished. On many there are still extensive stands of these, but it was not uncommon for the trees to be removed for purposes of construction in times past. Many were then planted with groves of coconut palms during a period when the oil of this nut had a high commercial value. This palm, *Cocos nucifera*, is a native of South East Asia to where it was restricted until man recognised its value. Then he transported it to countless, suitable and unsuitable places worldwide, to cultivate and harvest it. Sometimes this was straightforward, but such was the value of the trade that even quite unsuitable rocky islets of atolls many weeks away by sailing ship were used. Pits would be dug into the rock by armies of slaves and a relatively fertile mixture of earth placed in each. In each pit, one palm tree would then be grown. Whole atolls would be cleared for this, quite apart from expanses of high islands in tropical seas as well. When the trees began to produce, villages of slaves, and later on free-workers, would be employed to gather, husk and process the nuts. The valuable oil and copra would then be exported, except in those areas where piracy was a problem (which was most places), from where the less valuable whole nut was sent instead.

The heavy nuts of the *Cocos* tree may float some distance and when they fetch up on another shore they may self-seed. From the nuts of an initial few of these which colonise the perimeter of an uninhabited islet, more may later grow a little further inland. Today, an image of a palm-fringed beach may be the first scene to be envisaged by most of us when we think of coral islands but, except around its initial homeland, the palm tree is an introduction which has had enormous economic consequences but unfortunate side effects on the vegetation of many places.

A second introduction may also dominate the skyline of a coral island. This is the *Casuarina* tree, an evergreen, which can grow taller than the palm. Planted for its fast-growing wood, it proved to be very successful and, as its roots harbour a bacterium which fixes atmospheric nitrogen and thus produces fertiliser for the tree, it can thrive in soils which are too poor for many other plants. Then, when it becomes established, its needles form a carpet which inhibits other plants and the tree takes over the island. The ecological consequences of this tree too can be very harmful, despite its economic value in times past.

On the ground, the soil of the islands is mostly very thin. Old reef rock is exposed in many places and in others only grasses and herbs can grow. There is a constant flux in many areas between destructively-heavy downpours of rain which wash top-soil away and its gradual accumulation from dead vegetation. But, slowly, the vegetation on many islands attains some degree of permanence. Crabs beneath a forest of palms or native trees dig tunnels, continuously mixing the newer leaf litter through the sand, performing in a conspicuous way a useful activity that is more commonly done by the earthworm. Above them, birds make nests and add much nutrient to the soil in their droppings. Most will be seabirds— boobies, terns and frigates—all dependent on the fish of the reef beyond for food. By this means, some of the nutrients which were trapped on the reef are transferred to the island, replacing some of that which is washed away by rain. There is an energy and a chemical exchange here, too, showing that the island and the reef on which it sits are one.

Man

The ecosystem on a coral island is a small one, possibly the smallest that there is. The island's tiny size, its remoteness from other places and its stressful habitats and environment mean that few species ever reach it and of those which do, fewer still can live on it and colonise it. In very general terms, the more remote that an island is from the major, continental sources of life, the less are the chances that many species can or will make their way to live on the island. Also, the smaller the island is, the fewer are the number of species which can live on it in viable numbers. Yet, on most coral islands that have existed for a few centuries at least, there are usually a few species living in some semblance of balance, with every now and then a new arrival adding to the total and increasing the complexity of the ecosystem, or perhaps replacing something else already there. If an animal or plant is eradicated from an island it may be centuries before another member of the same species finds its way to the island to recolonise it. This depends a lot on the type of species concerned of course; it will be relatively easy for the wide-ranging frigate bird to recolonise should it be eliminated, but the chances of most land-bound animals finding a way back are remote indeed. Therefore, when man has colonised an island and stripped away much of its vegetation in order to plant coconut- or timber-producing trees, the changes are long-lasting at best and permanent at worst.

Such damage happened often in recent years, as commercial man extended his influence into the sea of coral to use islands for growing the produce demanded by people living in the temperate world. His effects were unfortunately not limited to replacement of the natural vegetation by groves of cultivated plants. For every stand of hardwood which he demolished, man also wiped out the homes of many

The sight of donkeys amongst the coconut groves may be attractive but is an artificial consequence of man's copra industry. These beasts of burden worked as hard as the slaves and, when man withdrew, because of the collapse of the trade, he turned the donkeys loose. Their grazing activity is not something which the island's ecosystem can absorb unnoticed.

kinds of animals and smaller plants as well. Most noticable of these were the birds which nested in the trees and shrubs and which, without a habitat, could no longer breed on the islands. But, for every tern and booby which was eliminated, several other smaller but equally important species went as well. The diversity of the islands fell drastically. Some of this waste could have been avoided. In many cases, the simple expedient of adequately feeding the slaves who unwillingly effected these changes would have meant that those unfortunate people would not have had to take the wildlife of the island to such a great extent. Birds and birds' eggs, turtles and turtles' eggs and the coconut crab by the thousand were taken on some islands as a vital supplement to the miserly ration given to the slaves by the owners of the new plantations.

And the impact did not stop there. Wherever he goes, man travels with his familiar ornamental and food-bearing plants and with a menagerie of alien animals. Most of his plants do not survive well on coral islands without a lot of attention, but some run wild with ease, and just one example is the leguminous ground cover plant, *Canavalia*. Where it gets a hold, it cannot be shifted. Man's animals, however, do worse. Rabbits, goats, donkeys, cats and dogs either add an unnaturally heavy grazing pressure onto the island plants or hunt ground-nesting birds. Rats, too, have accompanied man to the remotest islands where they have flourished. These animals, especially, have been accused of much damage—the plundering of birds' eggs for example. But whether they have caused more havoc than the cats and dogs in these fragile, small communities is doubtful and these co-travellers with man have probably received some of the blame due to the other animals because they are always unwelcome. They remain behind, however, and continue to cause damage when man and his pets move on.

In some cases, animals were introduced without man ever living on the island, to provide additional or emergency supplies of food for passing and stranded mariners in decades long past. Rabbits, chickens and goats have all served in this way, sometimes causing little havoc, sometimes a lot. The reasons for the introductions may be worthy, but the result to the island life has often been disastrous.

Given time to heal in the absence of man's activities or his alien introductions, the coral islands can slowly recover to some degree in many instances. Native plants and animals can recover in some parts at least. The coconut crab is seen again in greater numbers and in terrifyingly-large size on islands abandoned by man for a few decades. Turtles nest on beaches and colonies of birds roost again in returning stands of mixed vegetation and on the ground when the unfamiliar, overwhelming predators are removed. Societies of people, native to these kinds of islands for many centuries, live in a quasi-harmony with them, still very capable of causing destruction, especially when the population gets too big but, by and large, recognising the merits of a more harmonious existence within the frame of nature. Alas, western man who tries to live by a mistaken belief that he can subjugate nature, has had a different result.

When man brings his pets and rats to an island, the ground-nesting birds, like this masked booby chick (*top*), stand no chance, but when, on a coral island, the birds have not learned to fear man (*left*), then these enchanting places become no less than paradise.

Hawksbill turtle.

CODA

TODAY we know quite a lot about how a coral reef works. It is equally true that there is much more that we do not yet understand, for it is a built-in feature of science that every problem resolved brings to light further mysteries about the working of that problem and further ideas about what the key parts of it are. It is a part of the very nature of finding out that the more our knowledge grows, the greater becomes our awareness of our ignorance. This is a feature which has caused more than one philosopher to shake his head at the meaning of it.

One of the things we do know about a reef—any reef—is that it contains a particularly well-integrated system of life and one which is also closely integrated with the solid rock on which it sits. We know now that it is rarely possible to affect or damage one part without starting a follow-on effect into other parts of the living system because so many parts of it seem to be 'key' parts. The micro-organisms which recycle and synthesise nutrients, the red algae which happen to thrive and build in places too rough for anything else, the commensal crabs which protect their corals from being eaten, the zooxanthellae in the corals, and the corals themselves, are all essential. Many more species and connections will doubtlessly be shown in future to be equally important to the whole reef, and we need to find out in still greater depth exactly how it is that a coral reef works.

We need to know about these things for a good reason. We need to know how to live in harmony with the sea of coral and its contents, or else we may through accident and negligence destroy it. If this possibility seems too far-fetched, consider these statistics. At present throughout the world, two or three species are being forced into extinction every day and this is accelerating as the world's natural areas are being disrupted. It is estimated that more than one million species living now will be extinct by the end of the century, which is in 16 years time. Mostly these are land-based species because, until now, that has been where most damage has been done. It is harder to look at what is going on in the sea, but we know that already the rate of disappearance of some marine habitats is violent and with the habitats go the species.

Throughout life's history, species have been extinguished by other more successful ones and by being unadaptable to the earth's changing climate. Through the evolutionary process, more species have appeared and died than are here today. Some extinction therefore is natural and continuous. It has not been steady though. The usual background rate remains unknown but it cannot, on average, have been more than the rate of species appearance and that, we suspect, is very slow. Periodically, however, a great crash occurs. At least four have been recorded in past eons and these, as we saw much earlier in Figure 3, included marine reef-builders too. At these times reef-dwellers and reef-builders became extinct in droves.

Sea cucumber.

Today we are well into another crash, this time started by man. Although our telescoped sense of the history of the earth and its reefs suggests otherwise, the past crashes probably occurred over many thousands of years. Today's continuing crash, however, seems to be happening much faster than any of them and our own lifetimes will see the demise of a substantial proportion of all species. The impact that we are having on coral reefs is rising quickly too and those who have been observing them for many years all express alarm over the ease at which reefs can deteriorate.

If we are to know better how to stop this decline we must do two things. One is to find out much better how the reef works and where its weakest and its strongest links are. This could be relatively easy. Coral-reef research is very cheap indeed. Just a few hours' worth of military spending exceeds the whole world's reef research cost for the year. There is, of course, the problem of persuading people to provide this necessary cost and to think in terms of decades and of the distant future rather than the short term.

The other thing we need to do is much harder and this is to slow down the rate of thoughtless, irreversible destruction. Unfortunately, this is sometimes taken to mean conflict with industry or with the 'rights' of people to pursue activities of their choice in areas of their choice. Permitting this to happen can well deny others of their rights though and this is also a problem which has long troubled philosophers. In this category, there is another more difficult problem which concerns the short-term needs of many hard-pressed communities which live and use the coral sea in ways which now endanger the reefs.

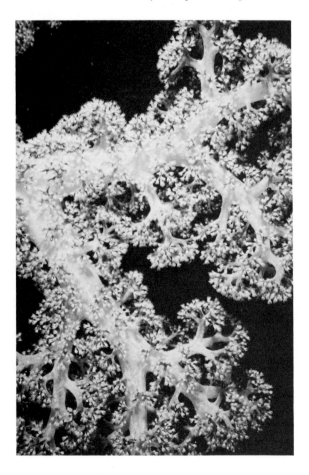

Dendronephthya—a soft coral.

Anemone.

143

Despite these difficulties, however, several nations have now made strong and successful moves to integrate all facets of human activity with the needs of the coral reef environment, to the long-term advancement of both. With luck and with political will—for it is now as much a political question as one of biological knowledge—we may be able to continue to see the benefits that we receive from the ancient, teeming, colourful world of a coral reef. Someone once said in reference to that other tropical wonderland, the rain forest, that its destruction, because of short-term negligence and profit, was like stripping a Rembrandt for its canvas. With a coral reef too, its assets are priceless and depend on it being and remaining a mosaic of connected form and living pattern.

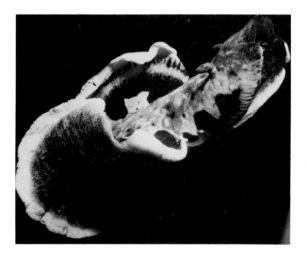

Spanish dancer—a nudibranch.

Patrolling.

BIBLIOGRAPHY

Two groups of references are listed for further reading: firstly general books on reefs and the biology and behaviour of their inhabitants and secondly a selection of 'reviews'. The latter are occasional articles summarising the new knowledge in this field and, for the serious layman and student, they provide the best entry into more advanced reading.

Books

Bellamy, D.J. (1979) *Half of Paradise* Cassell Ltd, London.

Bemert, G. and Ormond, R. (1981) *Red Sea Coral Reefs* Kegan Paul, London.

Bennett, I. (1971) *The Great Barrier Reef* Lansdowne Books, Melbourne.

Cousteau, J.-Y. (1977) *Life and Death in a Coral Sea* Cassell, London.

Faulkner, D. (1974) *This Living Reef* Quadrangle and New York Times, New York.

Faulkner, D. and Chesher, R. (1979) *Living Corals* Clarkson Potter, New York.

Fricke, H.W. (1973) *The Coral Seas* Putnam's (G.P.) Sons, New York.

Heatwole, H. (1981) *A Coral Island. The Story of One Tree Reef* Collins, Sydney.

Hopley, D. (1982) *The Geomorphology of the Great Barrier Reef. Quaternary Development of Coral Reefs* Wiley, Chichester.

Reviews

Borowitzka, M.A. (1981) 'Algae and grazing in coral reef ecosystems' *Endeavour* **5** pp. 99–106.

Buddemeier, R.W. and Kinzie, R.A. (1976) 'Coral growth' *Oceanogr. Mar. Biol. Ann. Rev.* **14** pp. 183–225.

Connell, J.H. (1973) 'Population ecology of reef building corals' In: Jones, O.A. and Endean, R. (eds) *Biology and Geology of Coral Reefs* **2** pp. 205–45. Academic Press, London.

Cribb, A.B. (1973) 'The algae of the Great Barrier Reef' In: Jones, O.A. and Endean, R. (eds) *Biology and Geology of Coral Reefs* **2** pp. 47–75. Academic Press, London.

Glynn, P.W. (1973) 'Aspects of the ecology of coral reefs in the Western Atlantic region' In: Jones, O.A. and Endean, R. (eds) *Biology and Geology of Coral Reefs* **2** pp. 271–324. Academic Press, London.

Goreau, T.F., Goreau, N.I. and Goreau, T.J. (1979) 'Corals and coral reefs' *Sci. Am.* **241** pp. 110–20.

Johansen, H.W. (1981) *Coralline Algae, a First Synthesis* CRC Press, Boca Raton, Florida.

Ladd, H.S. (1977) 'Types of coral reefs and their distribution' In: Jones, O.A. and Endean, R. (eds) *Biology and Geology of Coral Reefs* **4** pp. 1–19. Academic Press, London.

Lewis, J.B. (1977) 'Processes of organic production on coral reefs' *Biol. Rev.* **52** pp. 305–47.

Lewis, J.B. (1982) 'Coral reef ecosystems' In:

Longhurst, A.R. (ed.) *Analysis of Marine Ecosystems* pp. 127–58. Academic Press, London.

Loya, Y. and Rinkevich, B. (1980) 'Effects of oil pollution on coral reef communities' *Mar. Ecol. Prog. Ser.* **3** pp. 167–80.

Muscatine, L. (1973) 'Nutrition of corals' In: Jones, O.A. and Endean, R. (eds) *Biology and Geology of Coral Reefs* **2** pp. 77–115. Academic Press, London.

Patton, W.K. (1976) 'Animal associates of living reef corals' In: Jones, O.A. and Endean, R. (eds) *Biology and Geology of Coral Reefs* **3** pp. 1–36. Academic Press, London.

Rosen, B.R. (1981) 'The tropical high diversity enigma—the corals' eye view' In: Forey, P.L. (ed.) *Chance, Change and Challenge. The Evolving Biosphere* pp. 103–29. British Museum (Natural History) and Cambridge University Press.

Sheppard, C.R.C. (1982) 'Coral populations on reef slopes and their major controls' *Mar. Ecol. Prog. Ser.* **7** pp. 83–115.

Sorokin, Y.I. (1973) 'Microbiological aspects of the productivity of coral reefs' In: Jones, O.A. and Endean, R. (eds) *Biology and Geology of Coral Reefs* **2** pp. 17–45. Academic Press, London.

Steers, J.A. and Stoddart, D.R. (1977) 'The origin of fringing reefs, barrier reefs and atolls' In: Jones, O.A. and Endean, R. (eds) *Biology and Geology of Coral Reefs* **4** pp. 21–57. Academic Press, London.

Stoddart, D.R. (1973) 'Coral reefs: the last two million years' *Geography* **58** pp. 313–23.

Trench, R.K. (1976) 'Deposition of calcium carbonate skeletons by corals: an appraisal of physiological and ecological evidence' In: Drew, E.A., Lythgoe, J.N. and Woods, J.D. (eds) *Underwater Research* pp. 381–94. Academic Press, London.

Yonge, C.M. (1973) 'The nature of reef building (hermatypic) corals' *Bull. Mar. Sci.* **23** pp. 1–15.

Several other topics on aspects of coral reefs are covered by articles in the four volumes cited frequently above: *Biology and Geology of Coral Reefs* Jones, O.A. and Endean, R. (eds), Academic Press, London.

INDEX

Numbers in *italics* refer to black and white illustrations. Numbers in **bold** refer to colour plates. Species names are generally listed under their major group (eg. Algae, Corals) in alphabetical order with the common name (where present) preceding the taxonomic name.